GETTING TO OZ

Getting To Oz:

The Personal Journey Home to Your True Self

by Dr. Deborah Khoshaba

GETTING TO OZ:
THE PERSONAL JOURNEY HOME TO YOUR TRUE SELF

Copyright © 2014 Dr. Deborah Khoshaba

First Published in the United States 2014

Cover Art by Rebecca George
Cover Design by Ray Lundgren

Library of Congress CIP Information
Khoshaba, Deborah.
Getting to Oz:
The Personal Journey Home to Your True Self

FIRST EDITION

ISBN-13:
978-1502773210

ISBN-10:
150277321X

This book is dedicated to my beloved sister
Dorothy Khoshaba-Loughlin.
In her short 52 years on this earth,
she touched the hearts of everyone who knew her.
Love you, dear Dorth.

Until we meet again—Ching, Ching!

A heart is not judged by how much you love;
but by how much you are loved by others

—L. Frank Baum, *The Wonderful Wizard of Oz*

Table of Contents

FOREWORD

Getting to Oz is a culmination of Dr. Deborah Khoshaba's life and her 25-year career helping people to have the courage to face the stresses of living, and to forge a deeply meaningful life, no matter what the world throws at them. She inspires people with her warmth, wisdom, and encouraging ways.

Getting to Oz is not just wisdom expressed by an arm-chair philosopher. Deborah lives out what she maintains in this book and has forged a meaningful, rich life despite early hardships.

She knows first-hand how to show people the way to Oz, having counseled so many over the years and bringing her own learning to that process. Deborah walks the truth of the wisdom that there is nothing more fulfilling and meaningful than the personal journey we are privileged to have in this life. After all, life is, by its nature, stressful, and being able to learn from working on turning the stresses to developmental advantage is what life is all about.

This book is not only deep in helping you turn your stresses to personal advantage, but also provocatively and excitingly written. By reading the book, you learn how to unfold your true needs, desires, and talents. There is no one more equipped to help you in this than Dr. Deborah Khoshaba, whose life exemplifies the way to personal fulfillment. Throughout the years, Deborah has helped many clients to live more meaningful, happy lives.

I have worked with Deborah for more than 25 years, and feel so privileged to have experienced her extraordinary capabilities, from which I too have learned. This book is not only a great read, but through it you will find your way to your true life.

Salvatore R. Maddi, Ph.D.
Professor, University of California, Irvine
Fellow and Gold Medal Award Winner, American Psychological Association
Founder, Hardiness Institute

Acknowledgments

I am blessed to be able to write and publish my work to inspire others to do as I have—explore each facet of life experience and grow into an authentic self. It is my hope *Getting to Oz* will encourage readers to fulfill a purposeful life that is rich in meaning—a life worth living, no matter what must be overcome.

I've dedicated my own life to self-discovery, leaving no stone unturned. I've pursued each and every life happening that might lead me to the abilities, talents, and desires most true to my nature. In this sense, I've been in the process of writing this book all of my life. And, like Dorothy in *The Wonderful Wizard of Oz*, I have met up with people on my journey who have taught, encouraged, mentored, and inspired me to walk my own path. They have been nothing less than blessings in my life and I am pleased to acknowledge them here.

I'd first like to thank Wendy Lazear Werner, who collaborated with me on the writing of this book. I am blessed to have her as my mentor and friend. We meet up with many people on our journey through life, but just a handful of them are instrumental in helping us realize our dreams. Wendy is one of these individuals. *Getting to Oz* would not have happened without Wendy's creative brilliance and writing talent. She knew exactly how to bring my story to life, and how to integrate my personal and professional experiences and expert knowledge into a creative, coherent, and compelling narrative that would inspire readers. I will be forever grateful for her editorial talents. Perhaps, even more, I will value the positive, authentic experience of our collaboration. Our work together is something that I will forever look back on with awe, deep fondness, and appreciation. You are a blessing to me, dear Wendy.

I also want to thank the people who helped me prepare *Getting to Oz* for publication. First is my dear friend Jodi Renée Lester who copyedited the final version of this book and coordinated a team of stellar professionals to ready the book for the marketplace. Thank you for your invaluable help in this book's preparation. But most of all, I treasure our friendship through the years and the deeply meaningful ways in which it has evolved. Love you, my dear Jodi.

Thank you, John Palisano, for your eBook publishing expertise and making *Getting to Oz* available for hard copy and all the popular digital reading platforms. I also want to thank artist and founder of Chicago's The Art House, Rebecca George, for brilliantly capturing the theme of *Getting to Oz* in one beautiful and compelling image for the book cover. And last, but not least, I want to thank Ray Lundgren for bringing together all the elements of the book cover in a stunning design that surely will compel people to pick up the book and begin their magical journey to Oz. Each of you have contributed to the success of *Getting to Oz* and to my dream. Thank you!

Thank you to my sister Deana Khoshaba. She has rallied me through every twist and turn in my life, reminding me to never give up on my dreams. Love you, dear Deana.

I also want to honor my mother, Mabel Khoshaba, who has always been a major influence on me. By example, my mom taught me how to persevere in tough times and to never lose sight of my dreams. No matter how tough life got for us, my mother encouraged us to look ahead, do what we needed to do, and forge possibility out of our circumstances. Indeed, she is a *wonderful wizard of Oz* in the truest sense. I remember the first time I experienced her wizardry. It was a dark, financially tough time for our family. My mother knew we needed to feel uplifted and to have something to look forward to. She called us into a small sitting room. I sensed she had something important to tell us and sat glued to her side. With a writing pad and pen in hand she began to write a letter, reading its contents out loud as she wrote. The letter, written in her best broken English, was to Garry Moore, star of the then hugely popular *Garry Moore Show*. It described in detail her immigration to the United States and the struggles of her family thereafter. It went on to tell about her little ten-year-old girl named Debbie who had a very big singing voice and ended by asking if Debbie might audition for the show. When she was done writing, she carefully folded and placed the letter in an envelope, and told us she would mail it on her way to work the next morning.

As she wrote, I just sat in awe. *An audition to be on the* Garry Moore Show? Such a thing did not seem possible! But oh, did I dream over the following weeks! I'd excitedly run home every day and ask if *The Gary Moore Show* had written us back. My mother would smile and optimistically say, *"Not yet."* Then, one day, something amazing happened. She answered *yes* to my question! She handed me a typewritten letter (no computers in those days) that requested that we come to New York for an audition. Over the next several weeks, I looked at the letter over and over again to make sure it was true.

We never made it to New York. My parents' responsibilities and stresses did not permit it. Yet even though I never got to audition for Garry Moore, that letter had a profound influence on my development. I learned to have the courage to dream of possibilities "over the rainbow." And I learned that if I dared to realize my dreams, some of them might actually come true. Thank you, Mom, for teaching me how to turn adversity into opportunity, and to carry out my dreams with kindness, dignity, and grace. You are a true wizard. God bless you, Mom. Love, Deb.

I also want to express my love and gratitude to my husband, best friend, and business partner of twenty-five years, Salvatore R. Maddi. Thank you for your never-ending love, friendship, and support. Truly, *you* are my biggest fan. Many people verbalize their support, but you actually give it. Watching our dogs, helping out with the house, sitting and lovingly listening to my ideas and writings—these are just some of the ways you show me daily how much you love me and support my dreams. You are a blessing in my life, my love. Thank you for everything. God bless.

I want to thank all of the wonderful people who have sat across from me through the years and courageously shared the most intimate parts of their lives with me as their therapist. I am honored and grateful that our lives have intersected in this very special and intimate way. I have learned so much from each of you and feel blessed that you have allowed me to walk along side you, for just a time, on your life journeys. God bless.

And, last but not least, I want to thank all of my friends from *Psychology in Everyday Life*. You are the best. Your friendship and support means so much to me, and I am learning so much from all of you. I have learned that people from all over the world of every race, culture, religion, and country can be our friends if we drop our egos and connect out of the wisdom of our hearts. I've also learned that when we connect through our psychological rather than our social selves, it is amazing how similar we really are, no matter our apparent differences. Thank you for this blessing.

Experience is, for me, the highest authority. The touchstone of validity is my own experience. No other person's ideas, and none of my own ideas, are as authoritative as my experience. It is to experience that I must return again and again, to discover a closer approximation to truth as it is in the process of becoming in me.

—Carl Rogers, *On Becoming a Person*

Chapter One:

Inside the Tornado

First, I want to tell you a story. It may be one you know, but it is worth retelling, as it forms the basis of this book. As you read, I suggest you think about the powerful message this story carries. It is the reason this simple tale has inspired so many of us for more than a century:

> A girl named Dorothy runs away from home with her little dog Toto. She is swept up by a powerful tornado and deposited in a faraway place called Oz. At first she is frightened, and only wants someone to help her get back home. But despite her fears, she soon acclimates to her surroundings, making the most of any help that is offered. Joined by her new friends—a lion, a scarecrow, and a tin woodman— she makes her way along the yellow brick road to Oz, the home of a great and powerful wizard whom she believes will help her return home. In the end, she learns she does not need his help, or anyone else's. Going home is, and always has been, totally within her own power.

There are many positive messages in this simple story, but this one always stood out for me: *There is no place like home*. When I first read the story, I took this message at face value. But as I thought more about it, I realized that Dorothy's burning need was not for home in the traditional sense. After all, wasn't she running away from home, trying to find her own way in the world? Dorothy's destination was unclear to her, but she did have a burning desire to get there. Throughout the course of her journey she learned that home was much more than a physical place or a place we *come from*; home is a place we *aspire to* when we first begin to yearn for something more in our lives—whatever it is that lies *over the rainbow.* This is the home of our heart's desire.

Throughout this book, I refer to *going home* or *getting to Oz* as a journey to our true selves. *Home,* at least in the context of this book, means leaving behind the safe and familiar to find what is right for each of us. Getting to Oz is a journey of self-discovery that no one can make for us—not our relatives, not our friends, not our partners. To get to this new home requires that we leave the nest, a place of safety and security. The promise of this journey is what lies over the rainbow. What we find there is our true home, where we get to claim a life of fulfillment and meaning—the life that we were born to live.

Getting to Oz requires that we accept ourselves unconditionally, with all of our flaws and limitations. Where there is self-love there can be no pretense or delusion—only a clear and focused path to a happier and healthier life. We have to make a decision to love ourselves in order to take the first steps to selfhood on the road to Oz.

The Self in Question

The passage from safety and security to our new home begins for us as it did for Dorothy, "inside the tornado." Some crisis occurs that propels us forward, or some spirit rises up within us that forces us to move on. At first we may try to resist. It is difficult for us to move from the inherited identity passed down to us by our parents and their parents before them to an identity that encompasses our own values and beliefs, even if it is the right thing to do.

Inside the tornado refers to our initial fear—the panic that sets in when we realize we are alone for this journey and must let go of our attachments. At this first sense of loss and confusion, we may seek immediate safety and protection back home. But soon we realize there is no going back. If we persevere, we find ourselves in a landscape that seems both strange and familiar, just as Oz appeared to Dorothy. We are still a patched-up version of our parents' and society's expectations, but open to whatever comes.

After several twists and turns along the yellow brick road, we finally arrive in our very own version of Oz. The amazing winding path rewards us with self-knowledge—the realization of who we really are. It is something far different from what we can get by reaching back to the security of our childhoods.

Back at the Farm

Of course, where we come from is just as important as where we are heading. Our roots are the launching pad for self-discovery, the bow that launches the arrow as far as it will fly. We may not have an Auntie Em waiting for us back home, but for most of us, home and family are important to our past and to our future. Some of us are children of divorced parents, others have same-sex parents, and some of us may not know who our biological parents are. No matter our roots, whether we come from a poor or a rich family, a big or a small one, we all come from somewhere. More importantly, we all have some form of attachment to the security and safety of home.

When we are very young, we are grateful for this attachment; most of us are glad to be part of something greater than ourselves. With it comes a rich heritage of beliefs, ideas, and experiences that have been handed down to us through generations. Some of us come from close-knit families and feel a strong tie to our belief systems and values. Others are deeply attached, yet feel the urge to rebel, even when we are young, as if we didn't quite fit with our family's values or expectations.

As we grow we begin to stretch the bonds of attachment and to struggle to form a separate identity of our own. Even if our home lives contain challenging circumstances, and so many do, we still feel a sense of comfort in familiar surroundings. Yet we recognize that if we are to develop an independent life of our own, we need to break out and discover what we truly value and believe in. Metaphorically and physically, no matter how attached we are, like Dorothy, we all need to leave home.

Attachment

Attachment is one of the most powerful developmental structures that we will ever have, the foundation of our identity and an important indicator of our growth as individuals. Our attachment to family forms out of the blood we share and the preferences, values, and beliefs we pass on from generation to generation.

It's easy enough to know how attached we are to our loved ones—how much our identification with them means to us. All we have to do is reflect for a moment about what it would feel like to lose them, either through real physical separation or because we have rebelled against them in our ideas, beliefs, or values.

For most of us, feelings of anxiety and fear crop up when we contemplate this separation from home, even if it is of our own choosing. This anxiety lessens quickly, as long as we are provided adequate developmental experiences to explore our ever-widening environment. The healthy family unit does not close us in or shut us down. It encourages our independence, functioning as a developmental foundation that is secure and flexible enough to support our future self-explorations.

Picture a toddler learning how to walk. At first she holds on to tables and chairs so that she can begin to explore her world. If she does this on her own, without her mother or father rushing in to protect her from falling, she soon feels safe and secure, and is able to move farther and farther away from her base of protection, support, and love. In much the same way, we feel safe to explore our worlds because we know we can return home at any time, without fear of consequence. Our attachment to our family of origin is a *healthy* one. For us, family operates as a powerful fulcrum that both grounds us and lets us explore life without fear or hesitation.

But what if our attachment to home and family is insecure? What if, as children, we were over-protected and over-controlled? What if we were not allowed to fall without our parents rushing in to pick us up and protect us? If our parents are anxiously attached to us, we may find it difficult to explore emerging ideas, desires, and needs, and see where they take us. We in turn become anxiously attached to our families, needing their approval and fearing their criticism or rejection. We may worry that if we don't do as they say, their affection and love will be withheld from us.

It is healthy for children to approach life with curiosity and wonder, dreaming, as Dorothy did, of what lies over the rainbow. But dreaming doesn't come easily for the anxiously attached child who tends to see the world as a scary or overwhelming place. Instead of imaginings becoming the basis for self-discovery and exploration, they instead produce deep anxiety or disturbing dreams—a fear of what the future holds rather than a longing to embrace it.

When we are anxiously attached, we fear that the worst will happen rather than the best, and avoid opportunity and commitment. We fail to hear the cues from deep inside us that could lead us to a brighter future. They are drowned out by fears from long ago that continually surface in our minds. We may try to get past these barriers, only to find that we are terrified of the "big bad world." Caught in some internalized fairy tale that always predicts bad things will happen, we hide ourselves from the wicked witch, fearing the harm that may come to us. We may be safe and secure, but we miss out on life's adventures and the path to our true selves.

Anxious attachment may also lead us to avoidance or complacency. When we are anxiously attached, we may continue to maintain the status quo, hoping for change instead of allowing ourselves to create it. Lacking the inner trust and confidence that comes from a healthy and supportive home life, we foreclose on the chance to search out our true selves. For us, the journey to the authentic self is a challenging one, as it becomes difficult to separate the "me" from the "them," and to trust our own inner guidance system. Home for us is a weight that limits our progress as opposed to a basis for authentic development.

As parents, we can stop fear in its tracks by providing our children with healthy rather than anxious attachment. All of us have seeds of potential when planted in rich and nourishing soil. Healthy attachment allows a safe environment for children to try on various identities, like changes of clothing. If we encourage our child's freedom to explore, it won't stop the tornado from coming, but when it comes, our child will learn, sometimes through trial and error, how to hear his own voice above the roar.

The Ties That Bind Us

Anxious attachment is a special type of problem for those of us who are first-generation and immigrant parents, raising children in a culture different from our own. Perhaps we are afraid our children will grow up as strangers, culturally removed from us and disassociated from our values and beliefs. We may worry that this will weaken the ties that bind us.

And what about our children? It is possible that they may suffer a crisis of alienation—not knowing whether to adhere to our own rules and standards or to follow the norms of an adopted culture. This can be a real dilemma, especially if we sincerely want the best for them.

We have to strike a balance between letting go and encouraging an interest in roots and tradition. We have to show our children through our actions how it is possible to honor and preserve culture and identity, even if we do not wish to embrace it in quite the same way as our own parents did or their parents did before them. We do this not by pushing our children to conform to our own standards and beliefs, but by demonstrating through our own actions a love for our culture and heritage.

What we want to avoid at all costs is living through our children—hoping their successes will make up for our own failures and disappointments. When we force our children to succeed according to some plan we've dreamed up for them, we should not be surprised to see these dreams die on the vine. When our children fail according to our terms, the failure is even harder, for us and for them. This unfortunate pattern occurs just as frequently with parents who have economic, social, or psychological issues and fear they will be unable to provide a stable future for their children. Sadly, children are seen as the great hope for their parents, as opposed to unique and separate individuals with lives

6

and futures of their own.

If we are the children who grow up in such circumstances, it is important to notice how our parents may be contributing to our current frustration and unhappiness. Even if we believe we have been acting in our own best interest, we may be surprised to learn that we have been holding ourselves back, not wanting our progress in the world to threaten or cause harm to our parents, or add to their burden. It is a shock to find out that we may have limited our explorations to the avenues our parents suggested to us as right or appropriate, rather than risk hurting them. It is equally surprising to get the jolt that tells us something is not right with our lives—we have not been on our own paths after all.

The good news is, getting on the road to Oz helps us put a stop to the cycle of unhealthy attachment. Inside the tornado we are forced to come to terms with the ways in which old habits have held us back. We learn to use our attachment to home and family in healthy and productive ways and not let the past control or confound us. We learn how to be *of* our parents, but not live for them. Best of all, what we learn on the road to Oz helps us encourage our own children in the future so that these issues cannot be passed down to the next generation and the next. Getting to Oz releases us from the ties that bind in unhealthy ways, teaching us to preserve the past, but live our truth.

Breaking Free

No matter how we were raised, it can be difficult to find and follow our own true path. Even if we have a clear vision of ourselves, we may be reluctant to share that vision with our parents, especially if we suspect they will not be on board. Some of us want to have it both ways—to achieve what makes our parents happy and what we want for ourselves. Finding the balance may be tricky, especially sorting out our parents' wishes from our own. There are a lot of hopes, dreams, and expectations swirling around inside the tornado!

In my own case, I was, thankfully, able to balance out my dreams with my equally important goal of helping my parents. I knew from an early age that I wanted to become a singer. I also knew that if I did well in my singing career, I could earn enough money to help my parents achieve a better life. It was clear to me that I was fulfilling my own dream but at the same time helping my parents achieve theirs. I was not sacrificing my own goals for their sake—I was simply using a long-held dream of my own in a productive and morally responsible way. Achieving this level of good character was important to me, and just as much a part of my developing identity.

It is important to strike a balance between attachment and independence. Equally important is taking control over the process of becoming who we really are. To live authentically means we must take complete charge of our own lives. Whatever choices we make, we have to own those choices and not be afraid to go wherever they may lead us. In fact, throughout our lives, the choices we make *become us* as each step builds our identity and character, and shapes our future. Whether our dreams are forged out of our parents' hopes and losses, or those of our own, we must assume responsibility for the direction we choose.

Taking Our Place in the World

As individuals in a complex society, we have to form an identity—a structure of personality that gives us a place in the world. Attaining this identity is the process of unfolding our abilities and talents that are most true to who we are. Identity provides us with points of reference for thinking about short- and long-range experiences. We have an idea about who we may be, but we do not know for sure. We use methods of comparison and contrast to examine aspects of our lives that unfold before us. The task is not just to own our identity, but also to wear it well. We must know who we are, yet be flexible enough to grow and change as our lives develop.

Identity is what grounds us. By identifying ourselves with a certain race, culture, class, family, and gender, we stabilize our "operating system" and are thus able to move freely into the future. As the tornado swirls around us, our identity keeps us in the eye of the storm, strong and steady, confident of our place in the world. Whether it's Windows or Mac, we choose the operating system we live by, and we move forward, bracing ourselves for whatever comes.

Something Tells Me We're Not in Kansas Anymore

Suddenly, we are released from the tornado. Wherever we have landed, we know our lives will never be the same. When the tornado sets Dorothy down in Oz, she wakes up changed. She is still Dorothy, but a bolder, braver version of herself. She is shocked to learn she has, in fact, killed the villainous Wicked Witch of the East! Yet how is it possible? Who is this new person she has become, and how is she now capable of such an outrageous and courageous act? Dorothy hardly recognizes herself; but even though she is puzzled, she is not afraid. She looks around at the strange place in which she finds herself and tries to make the best of it.

When we first arrive in our own version of Oz, we may need time to adjust to our new surroundings. The winds of change deposit us exactly where we need to be; yet we may struggle to figure out where we are and how we fit in, even if we have painstakingly planned every step of our journey. We may try on different identities, jobs, friends, partners, until we find the right version of ourselves. This process of getting to Oz can takes months for some, years for others, depending upon our initial comfort level with ourselves and our degree of self-love. The key is to take control of the process and embrace whatever choices and challenges are made.

A Journey of Intention

What sets us on the road to Oz? For Dorothy, it took being knocked unconscious during a tornado! Hopefully, we won't need a jolt like that to set us off on our journey. The best way to get to Oz is to create a journey of intention—to take control of our lives so that self-motivation plus self-knowledge add up to self-fulfillment.

If we do need a push of some kind to get started on the road to the authentic self, that push is likely to come from our environment. Hopefully not from a fierce storm or some other catastrophic situation, but from some prompt or sign from the outer world. Perhaps it will be the comment of a friend, relative, or teacher, or an inspirational thought that comes to us during our daily walk—something privately taken in and held that spurs our imaginations and opens our hearts and minds to our true natures and talents. Yes, it can happen this way, too, and frequently does.

Dorothy's journey may seem accidental—the result of an act of nature over which she had little control. And yet, wasn't it Dorothy who made the choice to run away from home after the mean Miss Gulch threatened to take her dog away from her? It was this ability to stand up for her own principles that led her directly into the path of the tornado. Once swept up inside of the storm, she was forced to reckon with its terrible force—the force of an unconscious need for growth and change. When she looked inside the eye of that cyclone, what Dorothy saw there was her real self, longing to break free.

This is what happens to each of us whether or not we take the reins of our own self-discovery; the seeds of our potential, fighting to break free, ultimately win out, pushing us upward like flowers through the earth. Ready or not, we are forced to blossom and grow to our full potential. No matter what our fears, we begin to explore without and within, until we settle on a way of life that is right for us. Inside each of us, a tornado threatens to unleash its full force *unless we act first.* It's best if we can lead the way, acting with purpose and intention, rather than waiting for some jarring event to force us into the future.

Yet for many of us, it is too frightening to cut ties to what we know, even if it is doing us harm. We will do anything to fight off the pressure to grow and change, even choose alcohol or drugs to lull us into a false sense of security. We may hide behind damaging relationships that woo us with their promise of safety and security. We may become depressed or have eating disorders that temporarily distract us from what we were put on this planet to do. When we fall into these escapist behaviors, we become a lesser version of ourselves—copping out of life rather than living up to our full potential. These behaviors can be stopped once we face our fears and realize what is waiting for us in Oz. We can find a way forward.

Tuning In to the Sound of Our Own Voice

From the day we are born, we are shaped and molded by the sights and sounds of the world we live in. We hear many voices—those of our parents, teachers, siblings, friends, and strangers—urging us in every direction. Moreover, in recent years things have gotten worse. In the age of social media it is increasingly difficult to identify our own values and beliefs and then manage to hang on to them. Inside the tornado, confusion reigns. It is no wonder so many of us lose our way.

When we are young, we are especially vulnerable. Parents, teachers, and friends may suggest to us an education, job, or relationship path that is certain to make us happy. They want what is best for us and think they know the right route for us to take. On the surface, their suggestions sound reasonable. There is nothing wrong with finding a path in life that gives us social and economic stability, and also makes our loved ones and ourselves happy. It seems like a win-win no matter how we look at it.

But, not all roads that glitter are paved with gold. No matter how stable our life may seem to others, deep down we know that something is lacking. If we have not been living a life that we designed through our own imagination and effort, one day we wake up to find that we are miserable—that our lives are not at all what we want them to be. Many well-established, successful people enter psychotherapy at such times. They retrace the steps that have brought them to this point only to find that they did not consciously choose the life they have been living. Perhaps, for the first time, they begin to ask themselves questions about what it is they want and what type of life will make them truly happy.

Waking Up Inside the Tornado

There is a difference between wanting something to be true and believing that it can be. It is the awareness of real possibility that causes us to wake up inside the tornado. We are scared as hell, yet dizzy with possibility, now that we believe a fulfilling and authentic life is possible. This time we want to do our lives the right way, to rise above the swirling voices telling us to go this way and that, and to choose for ourselves a true and authentic path. *We want to find the road to Oz.*

To begin, we have to ask ourselves an important question: What is it that we want for ourselves—what will make us authentically happy? It is easier to buy into any old version of "the good life" if we have not yet examined what is good for us. This is a key point. Making a life does not subscribe to any specific plan of action, but to a plan that is the right fit for our own version of success. There is no singular right path to Oz, but there is a path that will fulfill us that is unlikely to fit anyone else we know. That is why it is so important to ask the question and then recognize the sound of our own voice in response.

It can be a shock to hear our own voice rising above the rest—assuming we are able to recognize it. When we do, we are forced to pay attention, to listen to what is true for us as opposed to all the others in our lives. This does not mean we reject all other influences; but we learn to discriminate and find our own truth. By recognizing and honoring the importance of the gifts we have inherited, they become the context in which we consider the ideas and opinions of others. This is key to establishing a strong sense of self. Once we make that vital connection, there are many other voices worth listening to. We can honor ourselves and still retain the connection we have to the world at large, including, of course, those closest to us.

Aaryan's Story

I first met 19-year-old Aaryan as his teacher at the University of California, Irvine. He wanted me to supervise a thesis paper he had written on the effects of sibling loss on surviving siblings. He theorized that personality resilience played a large part in one's ability to find meaning in the loss, which could essentially heal and move an individual forward again in life.

Just a month or two earlier, Aaryan had lost his eldest brother Rahul in a car crash. He had received the call from his older sister Radhika telling him to come home immediately. He arrived to find his parents collapsed on the floor, holding each other in limp arms and wailing with grief so palpable that it will remain a permanent fixture in his mind. For the first time in Arryan's young life, he was thrown inside the tornado as he came face to face with a tragedy that would change his life forever.

Aaryan was trying to find his way, but everything he had ever taken comfort in—the ideas, beliefs, and family doctrines prescribed by his Hindu heritage—seemed lost to him now. His role in the family was uncertain; his eldest brother was to have been the family savior—a medical doctor, like his father, who would care for his parents as they got old, guide his siblings when his parents passed, and carry on the family name through his offspring. But that brother was now dead, leaving Aaryan as the oldest male of his family. Now, nothing was certain.

I'm sure it was no coincidence that shortly after Rahul died, Aaryan signed up for my course in existential psychology. When we are inside the tornado, people and events often enter our lives at just the right moment to ferry us through life's underbelly. It seems that I was to be one of those people for Aaryan. He had no idea what the course was all about, but something told him to take it anyway, and he trusted his gut.

Existential Psychology was a course I had given many times before. Students loved it because it delved into the meaning of existence, focusing on authentic development and life choices. Aaryan seemed to love it, too. Twice a week I saw this eager young man with shining brown eyes sitting in the front row, hanging on my every word. It was obvious he was hungry to know. Week after week, Aaryan puzzled over a variety of issues he had never before contemplated. Grounded inside the tornado, he was able to focus on finding the answers that would help him move on.

That meant questioning everything he had held to be true, even if it meant facing family disapproval and rejection.

Slowly, Aaryan came to terms with the fact that the path his father had chosen for his eldest son—to become a medical doctor—did not suit him. Even more difficult, he pondered the nature of attachments, his own as well as others. Questioning his sexuality for the first time in his life, he came to accept the fact that he was gay. Once he found the truth inside of him there was no turning back. He did not become a medical doctor as his father had wished, but instead became a psychologist—a profession more in line with his true abilities, talents, and desires.

Like Aaryan, each of us must allow ourselves to get caught up in the whirlwind as we consider and examine all objectives that are put before us. This temporary confusion is all part of the remarkable journey to Oz, a place where we will meet the truest version of ourselves—not one that we create, but the one that has been there all along, waiting for us to come and claim it.

Ding Dong! The Witch Is Dead

When the tornado deposits Dorothy in a new land, she is shocked to be confronted by her own power. She professes that she is neither a good witch nor a bad witch, but just plain old Dorothy Gale from Kansas. Still striving to repress the new identity that has been handed to her, she struggles to accommodate it and do it justice. At this stage, she is not yet ready to grow; or she wants to, but isn't sure how to go about it.

This is the place we find ourselves when we get a glimmer of what might be waiting for us over the rainbow. We sense that we are now headed in the right direction, yet we aren't quite certain what to do with the identity we are leaving behind. Which part of our old selves do we kill off, and which part of ourselves do we keep? Exactly who is this new person we are striving to become? One of our great challenges as we make our way to Oz is understanding just how much is possible.

We Are the Decider

In the film *Dead Poet's Society,* John Keating, a professor at an English boarding school, leads his students on a compelling journey of self-exploration. Through the words of the great writers and poets, he holds the boys in rapt attention, instilling in their minds the romantic notion that they each must strive for the best version of themselves. The message in the film is that each of us has a voice that is uniquely ours to discover and use. But there is another cautionary message: We use this voice at a cost; should we fail to recognize what is right for us, we may get carried away by our excessive desire.

This is something to carry with us as we journey to Oz. We must always keep track of our true needs and desires, and not get so carried away that we think *all* things are possible. In truth, what is possible is only that which is possible for us as individuals. We set our own limits and decide for ourselves how far to go in whatever direction is open to us. We measure how far along we are on the road to Oz, not by anyone else's standards, but by our own; and we measure our progress, not by where we are, but by how far we've come. If we keep both of these things in mind, we will not be tempted to get ahead of ourselves and run the risk of losing too much of our identity.

We must also be aware that some of what we learn on the road to Oz may require us to make sacrifices. At critical times, we may reach a crossroad and have to decide which path to take: If we go this way, we may lose family or friends; if we go that way, we may keep our relationships but lessen our chance for authentic fulfillment. Do we want, like Icarus, to fly too close to the sun and risk getting burned? Only we can decide whether what we want is worth the sacrifice.

Sometimes on the road to Oz our self-exploration leads to an important discovery, such as Aaryan's discovery of his sexual identity. Here, there is no choice to be made; what we have learned is non-negotiable. Other emerging desires are equally compelling, but do require a choice. For example, through the years, many patients have asked me, "Should I divorce or stay in this marriage?" Here, our choice will require a sacrifice. Even if the choice is to stay in the marriage, we might be sacrificing our authenticity for the sake of preserving family unity. The important thing is that, on the road to Oz, we are the decider; we make the choice, always with our true needs and desires in mind.

On the road to Oz there are wonderful discoveries to be made, but also some painful ones. We must always be aware of the risks associated with this journey. These risks should be calculated so that we take them for the right reasons. Our over-arching goal is authenticity and truth. It isn't so much that we find exactly what is right for us, but that every step forward shows us more about who we really are. Ultimately, it is our journey, and we are in charge of every step we take. As we move along, we create the yellow brick road that forms before us. This is how our lives as whole individuals are created—with full awareness, one step at a time.

The Calling

As a young girl, I felt a constant yearning for the one thing I couldn't have—a safe and sheltering home life. I thought of home as a place where I would be protected and cradled with support, which is something my home never provided. I wouldn't just have walls, windows, and shelter; I would have nurture and support and something unknown to me: unconditional love. As so many do at this early age, I thought that home was all about the others in my life and how well (or not) they supported me. I had yet to trust myself to create my own sense of wellbeing.

As I matured, learned, and opened up my self-knowledge, I understood better what I had been searching for—not home in the traditional sense, but the comfort of living an authentic life. Gradually, I understood that others would never provide me with what I yearned for. I desperately needed to learn my truth and would be lost and searching—and I use "lost" in the most personal sense of the word—until I connected with my authentic self. This was something no one could do for me. Ultimately, I found my life purpose in showing others how to do this.

At some point in our lives, we are called upon to take a risk on ourselves, putting aside any fears we may have. The first leg of our road to Oz begins with this calling—and the burning need that arises to learn our truth. The goal is self-knowledge. We want to get clear about our identity and determine who we are as an individual, distinct from everyone else. Keeping our needs and goals in mind, and not allowing ourselves to go too far too fast, we begin the most important journey of our lives.

Chapter Two:

Lost in the Enchanted Forest

Each of us has the potential to wander into the enchanted forest at some point. One day our lives are filled with promise and hope; the next, we stumble and lose our way. Feelings of sadness, confusion, fear, and emptiness are common during this time. We may feel that life is hopeless. Depending on how we respond to this crisis, we either fall into a downward spiral or see it as an opportunity for growth and change.

Often, these confusing periods are triggered by some terrible misfortune—the loss of a loved one or a devastating illness. But sometimes confusion arises precisely at the moment when all of our dreams are about to come true. Just at the moment when the skies open up and bless us with their bounty, we suddenly feel as though we are on shaky and uncertain ground. *Are we sure this is what we really want? What we really need?* No matter what triggers this disorientation, we feel unable to stay the course.

It is in these moments of crisis that many of my clinical patients first come to see me. I assure them that once we work through the current difficulties, there is great hope for the future. The enchanted forest offers the opportunity for self-transformation. It is where we begin to separate what is unique to us from what is only borrowed or inherited from others—the authentic self from the social self. If we handle this passage well—and yes, it is a passage, with a way through to the other side—we have the possibility of learning to live again, this time in the best way possible. Lost in fog and darkness, we may hold on for dear life because that way feels safe and familiar. But total release into a brand new authentic way of life is truly possible at this time.

The Social Self

We arrive in the world without any knowledge, any consciousness, of our individual selves. Our whole world is made up of little more than our parents and siblings, and so many decisions are made for us. The first thing we become aware of at this stage is "the other," in the form of the people around us. Slowly, as we move out into the world, we find a need to adapt and the social self begins to take shape. Our five senses—sight, hearing, touch, smell, and taste—take in what is outside of us. Like petals of a flower, we naturally open outward to the world, and the social self is formed.

The social self is mainly a reflection of the world at large. Whether or not it is an expression of our talents and abilities depends upon the relationship between our immediate environment and our true desires and leanings. If the authentic you is a Picasso, but you are born into a family of entrepreneurs, your true self may have difficulty emerging. What we need from our families is much more than their approval; we need them to reflect what they see in us so we can see it clearly for ourselves.

All psychologists know that the social self we derive through parental and social norms is important to our development. We depend on shared ideas and values to make our way in the world. Identity with a social group functions as a necessary point of reference that lets us consider day-to-day experience against what we have come to believe and know. But this learning, although vital to development, can also become a block to unfolding our true purpose in life.

The enchanted forest represents a place of possibility. At last we have the chance to choose for our authentic self! It is difficult to leave behind what we know and what is familiar. We have to continuously remind ourselves that what we leave behind is only a *reflection of the world around us*, not our real self; it is a mask that keeps our true self hidden. When we drop the mask we begin to live with our whole being.

Enemies in the Enchanted Forest

As we make our way through the enchanted forest, there are three powerful and compelling forces that attempt to hold us back. These *enemies* are really our self-limiting behaviors that are within our power to change. They are not external forces, but internal traps of our own making—confused signals from our social self that prevent us from moving on.

The good news is we all have the ability to rise up against these forces and defeat them. Like the talking trees and flying monkeys that threatened Dorothy and her friends, they will do all they can to try and prevent us from succeeding. But as soon as we face them with our whole being, they will back down and let us pass. We will even be able to use these enemies to our advantage in surprising ways, thus hastening our journey to Oz.

Enemy #1: Fear

In my youth, I had a recurring dream. I was walking through the streets of Chicago and could not find my way home. It was foggy—the type of fog that is blinding. I walked tentatively, arms outstretched, with no ability to see anything beyond my next step. I held back, as if sensing an approaching cliff—but there was no cliff. Instead, I walked straight into a chain-link fence that prevented me from going any farther. This is how the dream always ended. Each time, I woke up trembling with fear.

Even as a young child I understood the meaning of this fear. I knew it reflected the stress of having grown up poor, with a father who gambled away nearly everything we had. I understood that the fog in my dream was a symbol of my disorientation and fear of the unknown; the chain-link fence was my mind's attempt to put a stop to what was happening. Or perhaps it represented my feelings of being trapped. Although I seemed to be desperately searching for something, it was never clear to me just what that something was. As I look back, I realize that my intuitive self was speaking to me. It was trying to help me find my way home.

We are all trying to come home—to ourselves. Although my dream mirrors the fear, uncertainty, and confusion of that time in my life, these feelings are all part of the process that takes place inside the enchanted forest. We take one tentative step forward then one step back, and we walk into chain-link fences, all in an effort to discover our own voice, our own way. We can shrink back from fear, returning to what we already know, or face our fears bravely and move on.

Our fear comes from knowing deep down that it is time for change—that something more is required of us—not the same old response, but one that comes from a true and honest version of ourselves.

No matter what has occurred that hurled us into the enchanted forest—a job far away from home, the loss of a loved one, personal illness—fear always accompanies change, positive and negative. Our pulse quickens and our hearts begin to race. Fear has alerted us to a crucial turning point in our lives. We're on unfamiliar ground—on the verge of a major breakthrough!

Of course, this is the moment when we most want to run and hide under the covers. Change is a scary prospect. We fear letting go of old attachments and ways of doing things. Even if the past no longer serves us, we fear the future. What if the possibilities disappoint us? What if we fail to live up to the demands of our true selves?

Yet we know retreat is not an option. It will only lead us right back to where we started. We all recognize the feeling—what happens when we take the easy road, pursuing a job that offers little challenge or a relationship that turns out to be yet another mistake. The familiar road isn't the least bit scary, *and that's precisely why we must avoid it.* In truth, if we're not feeling just a little bit challenged or afraid, then we're not on the road to Oz.

Fear mounts a potent defense, which is why we must fight back with an equally potent offense. We need to stand up to those *lions and tigers and bears* that challenge us in the forest of our imaginations. When our pulse quickens and our hearts begin to race—when panic sets in—that is precisely when we need to become focused and alert.

In the enchanted forest, we are finally able to face our fears instead of backing away from them. We move from the safety of the social self to self-knowledge—an understanding of what is possible for us in terms of authentic being. We start using our true gifts and talents, and suddenly our fear is gone. This is the moment when everything turns around for us. Defeating our fears, we find the route that points us toward home.

Enemy #2: Desire

The bestselling book *The Secret* showed readers how to manifest change in their lives. By using the law of attraction, we could attract health, wealth, and happiness. What a wonderful concept! But what if that life we wish for fails to take into account our natural gifts and talents? What if what we think is right for us is really just an expression of our social selves? We may run from one person, job, or activity to the next, trying to live up to our expressed need, only to end up far away from our true path.

When we find ourselves longing for what we lack, it's a sure sign that we are living through our social identity. As the Scarecrow, the Lion, and the Tin Woodman all came to realize, each of us has special gifts that can take us far—as long as we don't defeat ourselves by focusing on what we lack or filling the void with more things. Instead of always trying to attract more and better into our lives, we can dig deep within ourselves and find great potential for happiness and fulfillment.

Desire that springs from our social selves lands us in the deepest, darkest part of the enchanted forest where we are far from our centers. We should be very concerned when we think: "If only I had X, all my problems would be solved." The phrase "if only" is worrisome, and not just because what we think we want isn't within our reach. It may well be. But the time we devote to searching for it, and the deep and painful longing that accompanies it, prevents us from having any chance of developing an authentic life.

Moreover, in its most extreme form, desire can lead us into all kinds of negative states, such as addiction to alcohol, drugs, or food, or even criminal behavior. Such extreme and self-destructive behavior is a signal that we must step back and take a closer look at how social identity has led us astray. When desire is out of control, we need to examine its roots: the deeper issue we have with ourselves.

The good news is that it is possible to use desire in a productive way to bring about positive change in our lives. Like fear, desire can play a helpful role, pointing the way to recovery. First, we must reach back in our minds for internal cues. What led to our endless search for something external to fix our lives? Perhaps there is some unresolved issue—a feeling of deep inferiority or a lack of self-worth. To avoid the trap of filling emptiness with yet more emptiness, we must transform our unproductive *desire energy* into a force for self-growth and renewal. This is one of the most liberating steps we can take on the road to Oz.

Enemy #3: The Past

To move forward on the path to growth and fulfillment, we must first make peace with the past. In the enchanted forest, voices from the past have the power to confuse us—confronting us with our failures, making us feel ashamed, angry, or resentful. Our failure to let go of what has been, what others have done to us, or what we have done to ourselves, all contribute to our confused state of mind.

The past—represented in my dream by the chain-link fence—stops us from moving forward, keeping us stuck just where we are. It has its comforts, too; but even those can deter us, preventing us from taking chances or making bold choices for our lives. Fortunately, the enchanted forest is not just where we get lost; it is where we grow and heal and begin to reach out for future possibilities.

To move on to Oz we must free our hearts of bitterness and resentment; turn our broken hearts into open hearts and renew ourselves by starting over again—this time in the right direction. Whatever happened in the past, we must turn it into a learning experience for the future. We do this through open-mindedness rather than by dwelling on perceived wrongs or past mistakes. With open hearts, we are positioned well to bring into our lives the right circumstances and people to enrich us spiritually and emotionally.

We begin the process of letting go of the past by honoring it. That means valuing all of the lessons of the past, no matter how they affected us at the time. By claiming whatever anger, bitterness, or dislike we have toward others or ourselves, we are able to release these emotions and move forward with our lives.

A Prescription for Self-Love

Letting go of the past is best accomplished through the discipline of self-love. In the past, we may not have loved ourselves enough to follow our own hearts or protected ourselves in ways that were vital to unfolding our true purpose. We may have allowed others to take advantage of us or we may have failed to stick up for ourselves. We may have stayed too long in romantic relationships or jobs that were bad for us. Whatever we did that kept us stuck in the social self, we cannot find the way to Oz *until we let it go*. Getting to Oz requires that we bring our whole self on the journey.

Self-love gives us the inner confidence to open and unburden our hearts, and release any baggage from the past. As we do this, we begin to look clearly at ourselves and to build appreciation, deciding *for* rather than against our authentic selves. By learning to ignore any messages that threaten to pull us back, we focus all of our attention on what I call "authentic feeling and action." At the same time we see the value in all that has happened to us—the good and the bad. No longer are we victims of what happened long ago.

The lessons of the past are the building blocks for our new, more fulfilling life in Oz.

Living in the past keeps us trapped in the enchanted forest. Self-love gives us the strength and freedom to move forward. To help my patients with this process, I provide the following prescription for self-love. Used wisely, these seven rules enable us to find the gate in our own chain-link fence and walk on through to the other side.

Rules for Self-Love:

➢ ***Accept*** the past as learning that has brought you into the enchanted forest to prepare you for the road to Oz.

➢ ***Act*** to bring into your life what is psychologically good for you rather than what provides material or social reward in the moment.

➢ ***Say No*** to friendships, lovers, work, and activities that deplete or harm you physically, emotionally, and spiritually, or that poorly express who you are psychologically.

➢ ***Live Intentionally*** with design and purpose. Get on the road to Oz. Even if you don't know where you are going, just the intention of taking the road to Oz is enough to keep your eye on the journey that will get you there. With each step forward, you leave the past behind, appreciating all that it did to bring you to where you are in this moment.

➢ ***Recognize*** that you alone are responsible for your choices.

➢ ***Trust*** in the future, because you have yourself.

➢ ***Honor*** authentic fulfillment as your chief life purpose.

The Path to Mindfulness

When we become lost in the enchanted forest, we are more in touch with the present moment than we have ever been. Having let go of our social identity, we are now willing and able to bring our whole self into our life choices. By making mindful choices, we easily connect with our intuitive self and see clearly the road we are meant to follow.

What is mindfulness? Many of us are familiar with the subject from having practiced yoga or other disciplines to help us achieve this focused state. But we don't need years of meditation and contemplation to achieve a conscious way of life. We can eat an apple, or we can eat an apple *mindfully*, appreciating its juiciness, enjoying its texture on our tongues. Mindfulness is an instinctive choice that we make when we commit ourselves to experiencing life with our whole being.

A Lucky Break

It was a crisis that led me on my own path to mindfulness. I was twenty-one years old, married for just over a year. I was singing with the Chicago Lyric Opera as a company singer. Life was going well, and I thought I had everything I wanted. Then, overnight, my fairy tale life turned into a nightmare. I didn't know it then, but what was about to happen would become one of the most important turning points of my life.

My downward slide began with the discovery that the older, handsome, successful man I had married was an alcoholic. Over time, he became mean and abusive, and it gradually dawned on me that I was *sleeping with the enemy*. Although I had let my youthful naiveté and social self draw me to this type of man, I finally found the strength to leave the marriage. But at the age of twenty-two, armed with only a couple years of music education and a boatload of pain, I felt emotionally and physically broken. My marriage had been a failure, and without the finances to see it through, a professional operatic career was no longer viable.

Had my childhood dream been prophetic? I certainly felt as if I was lost in the fog—a fog of great confusion and despair. With only myself to count on, I tried to move forward. But just as in my dream, I seemed to run into one chain-link fence after another. All paths were closed to me. At least, this is how it seemed at the time. *What did I want? What should I do?* If there were signs, I could not read them to find my way out of the forest—at least not with the tools I had at my disposal. The chain-link fence that once woke me from a nightmare was now an impasse that I could not break through.

Then came the moment that would change my life. I was sitting in my parents' backyard on a warm summer day. The strong hum of the air conditioning unit behind the house became a mantra, pulling me inward and silencing my mind. I was paying attention, grounded deeply in the present moment that contained my entire past and my future. A fountain of ideas, images, and feelings spontaneously sprang upward from inside of me. I was present to each and every one of them.

This was when it came to me—a thought so vivid and powerful that it commanded my full attention. *Debbie, you will become a psychologist.* And yes, the chain-link fence popped into view, but this time with an unlatched gate that I could open and walk right on through. By doing this, by accepting this gut feeling, I opened myself up to what was my authentic life path. I did not know how I would bring it about. I just knew that it was the right path to follow—my way out of the blinding fog.

My moment of clarity was nothing short of a lucky break. It was the hum of the air conditioner that led me into a pattern of deep breathing—something I had learned to do during my training as a singer. At the time, I had no idea about mindfulness and could not understand how it had come to me. It was only later, when I thought about the extraordinary clarity that had come to me that day, that I realized the power of deep breathing and mindfulness to change lives.

I know now that what I heard that day in my parents' backyard was the voice of my authentic self—perhaps for the very first time. It was only much later that I began to understand the power of mindfulness to change lives. I realized that it was possible to create mindfulness just by getting past our automatic responses to life, and by using a simple but powerful tool to create a purposeful and conscious state of mind.

Three Steps to a Quiet Mind

On a daily basis, most of us function using automatic thinking: Our rote activities—work, running errands, fixing flat tires, grocery shopping—require little, if any, deep thought. Even when we perform more complex tasks or solve daily problems, we use set rules and routines that close us down to ideas, feelings, and gut hunches just outside our focus. We may feel as if we are fully aware and wholly functioning, when in fact we are using only a tiny portion of our faculties.

For the purposes of going about our daily lives, automatic thinking is a necessity. It would be hard to carry out daily responsibilities if we had to give deep thought to each one of them. And yet, some problems require more of us, especially problems relating to self-development. These problems can't be handled on autopilot because we have no precedent for understanding them. To work through these challenging issues, we need a tool that will help us tune out our social self and tune in to our authentic self. That tool is "deep breathing."

Isn't it amazing that something as simple as deep breathing could be such a powerful tool for self-development? Yet it is. Deep breathing takes us from automatic thinking to mindful experiencing. Our field of awareness expands greatly as relaxation unites our bodies with our mind so that all of experience is open to us. We temporarily suspend reasoning and judging, and instead experience ideas, feelings, and gut intuitions that connect us to the moment. This is mindful experiencing. Like the wizard's crystal ball, it allows us to view the whole of our experiences, connecting us to all of our past and our future.

There are three simple steps to a deep breathing practice. Let's get started.

Step One: Alternate Nostril Breathing

This is one of the best breathing techniques to deepen breathing, calm the mind and nervous system, direct attention inward, and balance the *thinking* (left) and *feeling* (right) hemispheres of the brain. Just five minutes of alternate nostril breathing gives optimum creativity and opens us to gut hunches that express true desires and needs.

Each cycle of breathing is made up of one lungful of air that is inhaled through one nostril and then exhaled through the other. Begin with five cycles of breathing. Once you get the hang of it, carry out breathing cycles for at least five minutes. This will balance the nervous system, turn you inward, and expand awareness.

Are you ready? Cycle One: Close off the right nostril with the ring or index finger and inhale slowly through the left. Hold to a count of four, then exhale the breath fully through the right nostril. Then, close off the left nostril with the ring or index finger and inhale slowly through the right. Hold the breath to a count of three or four, then exhale the breath fully through the left nostril. This completes one cycle of breathing. Do this for five cycles until you get the hang of it, then increase this exercise to ten cycles of breathing.

Step Two: Mindful Awareness

As our deep breathing begins to relax us, we become mindfully aware of everything that comes into our field of vision. A vast space opens up as our field of awareness expands and contracts with each breath. In observation mode, we note the rise and fall of each new idea, feeling, and intuition. We let the idea, hunch, or image come to us, but we do not get lost in it. At this point, we are only observers and do not try to understand or evaluate the messages that come to us. This non-interference and non-judgment quiets the mind.

We continue to relax and take everything in for as long as necessary or until we feel comfortable. By not permitting ourselves to control or think for an extended period, we begin to sense the joy of quiet observation. We continue to watch in a non-judgmental way as each kernel of an idea pops into our field of awareness, then disappears from view. This is a new experience for most of us, just as most things are on the road to Oz.

Step Three: Interpretation

From this liberating state of mindful awareness, we move into the next stage where we interpret the meaning of our internal messages. Deep breathing has allowed our authentic voice to speak to us. Now we must figure out what it was trying to say.

As we think back to the experience, we search for a word, phrase, or image that brought us an isolated moment of clarity.

What meaning can we take away from that moment? It is possible that we will have to string together several such moments to make sense of them. The awakening to the authentic self comes in its own time, in its own way.

How Breathing Works

We have four main body systems—autonomic (responsible for brain and body arousal, immune (responsible for immunity and defense), endocrine (responsible for blood sugar management, and the gut (responsible for our digestive processes). All of these systems are interrelated as they are all extensions of the mind. The brain uses information it receives through all of these bodily processes to interpret our stress level, which includes an evaluation of our breathing rate, posture, and muscle tension.

The brain *decides* to activate the fight-or-flight stress response for any activity that involves brain and body arousal, like working, running errands and even socializing. This is an intricate chemical process that increases the firing of nerves and causes the body's messengers (hormones) to tell the muscles to dump stored fat and sugar into the bloodstream. Suddenly, we have much greater energy, as natural steroid hormones like Cortisol are released, acting like shock absorbers to raise our tolerance for pain. While this is happening, the immune and digestive systems temporarily shut down so that all of the body's resources are focused in only two directions: fight or flight.

The trouble is this fight or flight mode doesn't help us at all when it comes to fulfilling our deeper needs. The fast brain wave activity that is a result of the stress response produces a narrow field of awareness, causing us to focus solely on linear, reasoned information. Not only are we unimaginative in this state, we also rely strictly on rules and routines to solve our problems. What is more, the gut has temporarily shut down to activate the fight-or-flight response. As a result, ideas, images, and hunches arising from the gut are now completely unavailable to us.

You may have thought the term "gut hunch" was just an expression and be surprised to learn that the gut is actually a nervous system on its own. It has its own neurotransmitters that respond to and remember experiences, providing a physiological basis for intuition and gut feelings. The understandings and intuitions that we need to help us find our ways out of the enchanted forest live inside our gut. We just have to know how to access these deep and powerful hunches—and to bring them forward so that we are able to act on them.

Deep breathing provides the answer. Remember, the brain pays attention to this activity. When breathing slows, the brain shuts off fight-or-flight activation and all of the biochemical activities that support it. Nerve firing is reduced so that every nervous system becomes functional once again. Brain waves slow down, opening us to our full mental faculties and an ever-expanding field of awareness. We connect with understandings, ideas, images, and hunches that arise from deep inside of us. Deep breathing has brought us to a state of mindfulness.

Putting It All Together

The gut hunches that arrive during our practice of mindfulness may seem to come from out of nowhere, when in fact they have been with us much longer than we know. Not only are these hunches creatively linked to our past, but they contain valuable information about our future. Perhaps it is difficult to accept that the whole mind can actually bring these messages to the surface. But I believe there is a knowing force in each of us that is stronger than our ability to silence it. When we quiet our minds, this knowing force shoots everything that has ever happened to us into our full awareness. If we stay long enough with a gut hunch, the mind, using its full faculties, continues to combine and recombine our life experiences into new meanings open to our interpretation.

For example, in the dream of my childhood, the fence was a comfort to me, a known point of reference in the blinding fog. I welcomed its protection in that confusing time. Once I became mindfully aware, I no longer needed this protection; instead, I found the courage to follow my heart and mind. Because I was ready to hear my authentic voice, my "security fence" turned into a gateway to my future—a direct path to my true self.

Fortunately, that day in my parents' backyard, despite knowing that something important had just happened to me, I allowed myself time to sit with my new idea, time to put it all together. I did not cast off my feelings and intuitions as implausible. I did not question, criticize, or evaluate my sudden insight that I should become a professional psychologist. Nor did I think about whether it was possible to actually make it happen. I let the idea develop inside of me. I went with it until I discovered its meaning in my life.

Leaving the Enchanted Forest

We emerge from the enchanted forest with the knowledge that we have the power to change our lives for the better. We realize that this road we are on is our very own creation—a purposeful path and the next leg of a painful but important process. We instinctively recognize this path as our own, as no two paths to Oz are alike.

At first, we may feel unsteady on our feet. Maybe we're even afraid, but our fear has a purpose; it slows us down some and heightens our senses to the sights, sounds, and smells all around us. As we move along, we find ourselves picking up the pace. The ground beneath our feet is still new to us; yet it is also strangely familiar. Our instincts are on high alert. We screen out any anxiety we may have about the future. We are so in tune with ourselves in the present moment that we are able to defeat any forces that try to challenge us or prevent us from moving forward.

In our new state of mindfulness, we are able to fight off any remaining self-doubt or self-limiting behaviors. We are well on our way to Oz, but realize there will be many more choices to make and much learning to do. Yet as we continue to live our lives in a mindful, conscious way, we immediately start to see an improvement in the way we feel about ourselves. We go from feeling weak to enlivened, uninterested to curious, uninspired to creative, and unimaginative to resourceful. Likewise, we notice that we are more understanding, patient, and kind, open to the needs and desires of other individuals. Our new awareness makes available many of the avenues that were previously closed to us. We live fully and deliberately as we stay connected to our true self.

Getting to Oz requires us to continue unfolding ourselves, consciously and authentically. As the journey progresses, we continue to change, over and over, each time it is asked of us. When we turn a crystal in our hands, the angle of light passing through it changes, causing the way it catches and emits light to change. Similarly, when we connect with our true self, the light of our passion changes, causing the way we draw it in and reflect it to change as well.

I promise you that all of this is achievable. All we have to do now is turn on our inner GPS, grab the steering wheel, and set the course for Oz. Once there, we will be able to move away from relying on distinctions made in the past, allowing a brighter future to emerge. When we engage with our whole being, we are investing in ourselves, making a life and not just a living. We leave the enchanted forest far behind, determined to live our life mindfully, as a whole being, ready for the next leg of our journey.

Chapter Three:

The Yellow Brick Road

The yellow brick road that takes us to Oz is a miracle of our own creation. It is our road, our way, paved by the choices we make and the goals we have set for ourselves. This is an intensely personal journey, unlike anything we have ever read about in a book or seen in a movie. The Oz we discover is the one that is meant strictly for us—our very own version of what is possible and what fulfills us.

We all want to have a fulfilling life, but sometimes the space between wishing and actually getting is vast and vague. How do we shorten the gap? We do it by paving the yellow brick road, brick by brick. A continual honest expression of who and what we are gives definition and structure to our dreams, allowing us to materialize what is in our hearts and minds.

On the road to Oz, we will sometimes take big risks, paving a road that challenges us and sometimes moves us in bold new directions. As a result, some doors may close to us forever, but new ones open. This is the nature of this marvelous journey—with surprises and setbacks, but also vast rewards for our effort.

Paving Our Way to Oz

We arrive at the yellow brick road hopeful. We want our dreams to be fulfilled, our lives renewed. We begin with our own set of expectations, values, and intentions, using all the skills at our disposal to determine what we are capable of and how far we can go.

At first we use only our known skills and talents—the sum of all our experiences in life thus far. But as we build confidence along our self-created path, strengths and talents we didn't know we had begin to emerge. We discover things about ourselves that boost our self-confidence, raising the ante and giving us hope that we can achieve everything we want in life on our own terms.

When I speak of paving our way to Oz, what I really mean is having a plan and a purpose. To set an intentional path to Oz, we need to do more than just hope for the best. Even if we aren't one hundred percent certain about our goals, we don't stand still; we move toward what we intuit is right for us. Think of it as plotting a route on MapQuest or Google Maps, with a starting point and a destination. We begin by asking for the shortest, most beneficial route. We then identify the possibilities (based on our strengths, desires, and unrealized talents) and consider their probability relative to what we know (possible limitations). This is how we create a personal map that allows us to move forward.

Of course, even a computer can't tell us everything we will encounter on the day of our journey. Once en route to Oz we can expect to encounter many things that surprise us, including new versions of ourselves. We may uncover skills we had no idea we possessed. We may be surprised to find that the things we most wanted (a brain, a heart, courage) were ours all along. It took functioning authentically in the world (paving the road) to take advantage of these talents and capabilities. We must try to make the most of each new gift as it is revealed to us.

We all have a unique contribution to make in this world, and this journey will help us to discover it. Like the Scarecrow, the Tin Woodman, and the Lion, we learn that whenever we want more from life we must not be afraid to speak up. Declaring what we need and then going after it helps ensure that our wishes will be granted. There is no better route to self-fulfillment than making the most of our lives.

The yellow brick road will unlock great secrets for us if we are willing to actively pursue our dreams. If we can give life all we've got and manage to stay on the intended path despite our setbacks, our creativity and determination will be rewarded—with our very own pot of gold at the end of the rainbow.

The Open Road

We are all invited to take the journey to Oz. We start out with no restrictions, no questions asked. Who we are and where we come from has no bearing on this remarkable journey, except as a basis for our own future growth and development. The yellow brick road does not discriminate; it is open to everyone, yet each of us is an individual with a unique path.

We begin as a compilation of our past experiences—a jumble of ideas and reference points that have been accumulated over the years from others in our lives. But quickly we move on, because we recognize there is something we must discover about ourselves, someone we were born to be. On the yellow brick road we are no longer limited by our past. Our lives are finally up to us.

The Searchers

The first thing we are asked is to take a chance on ourselves—to be willing to find out who we are through our experiences in the world. In exchange we are offered the opportunity to be delivered to our true purpose. We accept the offer, hoping the truth will empower us and set us free to live an authentic life.

We want to be free—free from attachment to things that are no longer good for us, free from the restrictions of the past, free from the goals that were set for us as opposed to those we set for ourselves, and even free from our own self-imposed judgments and limitations. As we become mindful of the true state of our being, independence becomes a real possibility for us—synonymous with who and what we really are. We have thrown the door to our soul wide open.

Like Dorothy and her companions, we are solo travelers in a new world. We might even compare ourselves to the cowboy hero of the Old West riding into town on his horse—a lonesome drifter who has been striving to make his way in the world. We may have friends, colleagues, and family, yet we ride solo, our hat pitched forward to conceal our identity as we shield our eyes from the sun. Like John Wayne in the classic film *The Searchers*, we are on a mission to protect and defend—in our case, our identity—and nothing can thwart our plan.

Yes, the journey is tough at times; but our longing for

36

independence and growth keeps us focused. Like the Scarecrow, the Tin Woodman, and the Lion, we each want something that is uniquely personal to us—some driving dream or hope that keeps us moving forward on the road to Oz. We need to remain mindful of these goals and hold our heads high. We have nothing to fear and nothing to apologize for; the journey to find ourselves is a proud and noble one.

When we create the independent road of our dreams using our hearts, minds, and courage, our confidence soars. As we do things in the world to prove our worth, we carve out a path that belongs only to us, a zigzag map of independent ideas and bright promises that frees us at last to be ourselves.

The Gift of Disadvantage

We all start out the journey to Oz at square one—but that square is different for each of us. Some of us begin our adult lives with more than others—more money, more support, more of what seems like a chance in life. We may have grown up in large homes surrounded by loving and prosperous families who supported and encouraged us, while others came from dire poverty with no one to lean on when times got tough.

In treating my clinical patients, I have noticed over the years how a difference in early life circumstances creates a difference in outlook and perspective. Those who have experienced disadvantages, such as poverty or illness, have been weakened by their sufferings. Loss after loss has given them much more than they have the right to bear. These individuals arrive in therapy alive but not living. Starting out with such deprivation, it does not seem possible that they will have enough strength or skill to make the journey to their authentic self, or that they will even care to try.

And yet, many of them do try, and many of them succeed. The truth is, when it comes to finding happiness and fulfillment, having *more* and *better* doesn't always put us in the best starting position. Those who have suffered the most usually find it easier to let go of the past and are therefore freer to take the journey to Oz. Starting out with less also tends to limit our expectations, so we are less likely to be disappointed when things don't go our way. When we have so little to lose, we have everything to gain. The gift of disadvantage often strengthens our intention to travel the road to Oz.

The great personality theorist Alfred Adler wrote that healthy living consists of succeeding in our effort to strengthen our shortcomings so that we are able to carry out the life we've imagined for ourselves. When it comes to finding our way to Oz, past failure may be our best ally. Many things are possible when we fail once or even multiple times and have to keep on trying until we break through some barrier. Once we see an opening for self-improvement, we are encouraged to develop and grow our life in deeply meaningful ways.

Reinventing the Possibilities

My own life is a good example of the gift of disadvantage. When at the age of twenty-two I was forced to let go of my dream of becoming a professional opera singer, I thought my life was over. The only dream I'd ever known was dead on the vine.

Who am I, if I'm not a singer?

Then one day I realized that no matter what I had imagined for myself, life had other plans for me. I had to face my fears and insecurities; otherwise, I'd be stuck forever, unable to move on. Adler writes that our insecurities may be signposts urging us to move our lives forward. I believe this was true for me, and fortunately I followed those signposts.

It meant ten long years of training, but I followed the route that mindfulness dictated, earning my degree in psychology. During those ten years, I discovered desires, talents, and abilities I didn't know I had. But perhaps, more than anything else, I learned something very precious about life. I learned that by working through our insecurities and strengthening our apparent weaknesses, we have the chance to reconfigure the best life we can imagine. I put myself squarely on the yellow brick road. It was the best thing I ever did.

True Grit

Whether our early circumstances in life were advantageous or not, we must try to make the most of them. When it comes to Oz, we are the guardians of our fate. To pave our authentic road with true intention, we have to keep our head down, our mind focused, and our heart engaged.

We won't reach Oz by looking all around and thinking about who has more than we do. The key to finding our truth is to stabilize as much as possible, which means focusing on our own truth and no one else's. When we view ourselves in comparison to others, we dampen our enthusiasm for change and diminish our possibilities. We need to see any perceived disadvantages as door openers, so that our lives progress in timely and fortuitous ways.

If you doubt this, think of those who have done well in life regardless of their early circumstances—people like Bill Clinton or Pakistani schoolgirl Malala Yousafzai, two individuals who faced different types of adversity at a young age and triumphed. Think of Aimee Copeland, who lost hands and legs to a flesh-eating disease but rose above this challenge. These are individuals who came to the yellow brick road with little else but their own cleverness, determination, and courage. Dig deeper into history and ponder the life of Abraham Lincoln or Albert Einstein, two great men who suffered their whole lives with clinical depression. There are many such stories of individuals who made the best of difficult life circumstances, setting appropriate goals for themselves and, in so doing, reinventing their possibilities and repaving their road to Oz.

Course Corrections

I don't mean to imply that everything is possible. Life does have its limits, regardless of our starting point or capabilities. But all of us have to discern what is possible in relation to the givens of our lives. No, we can't all become president of a country or a college or even of our class at school. We might not have the skills to become a doctor or a lawyer or a carpenter or an astronaut. Some of our desires may not be realistic in light of our innate skills and capabilities.

The yellow brick road to Oz challenges us to distinguish what is possible from what may never be. We must be honest with ourselves in setting goals that are achievable. This is both our task and the reward of making this journey. It does us no good to long for what we may never be able to obtain. Realism and an awareness of our true talents and abilities are called for. Setting realistic goals makes it possible for us to transform our hopes and wishes into a practical manifestation of our true needs.

Even if we set realistic goals, it is possible to fall short of our expectations. If this happens, we must not blame ourselves. Instead, all we have to do is make a course correction that gets us back on track. We are continually challenged in this way on the yellow brick road. As engineers of our destiny, we set the course that favors our wellbeing and make any adjustments needed without judgment or self-criticism. We are only human beings, after all.

If I Only Had a Brain (a Heart, Courage)

Striving, longing, wishing, and hoping! It is our dreams that send us off on the yellow brick road. They provide the momentum that gets us going and makes it possible for us to move from a place of stasis to somewhere over the rainbow,where at last we can function as our true self.

Our dreams may take us to imaginary places that we have never seen before. We look at our glass as half full and long to fill it by bringing our whole being into the world. Our optimism carries us forward. Other times we get into "if only" thinking, focusing only on the things we lack: A brain, a heart, courage. This is when see our glass as half empty and worry that our problems are too big to solve. Negative or even catastrophic thinking may keep us from unlocking our potential.

But once on the yellow brick road our eyes are opened. The force of our longing transforms us and we see the truth about ourselves unfolding before our eyes. The Scarecrow's cleverness saved the group from treachery time after time; the Tin

Woodman's heart was always on display in his kind treatment of his fellow travelers; and the Lion's courage enabled him to jump in as needed to save the entire group from disaster. When we use our true potential out in the world, we no longer focus on the things we lack. Using our abilities is the root of self-affirmation. It gives form and substance to the dream and lights up our path to Oz.

Walking down the yellow brick road is about making the best possible use of our talents and capabilities. For many of us this is easier said than done. How do we know what we have and who we are? We begin by recognizing the contributions we have made to our own lives and the lives of others. We invest in ourselves, day after day, using our best traits and valuing them. We do not hide our talents, expecting others to draw us out. Life is not a game of hide-and-seek. Nor do we look for others to complete us. We work one step at a time with what we have been given, even if it isn't exactly what we think we want. Growth and possibilities emerge in countless ways when we stop the longing and start the living.

Yet the longing is essential, as it starts us on the road. First we dream; then we build. Then, whatever it is that we long for (my becoming a psychologist, for example) becomes a beacon that guides us forward. We follow the light of our hopes and dreams until they take us where we most need to be. Fear evaporates. Things fall into place. Progress is made, as we begin to manifest our true selves.

All That Glitters

We all know about the destructive force of jealousy. This is not so much about longing for what we lack as it is about longing for what others have. We're walking down the street feeling pretty good about ourselves, when we happen to look over at someone's designer suit or shoes, and suddenly our own clothes pale by comparison. Or we're at a company party and overhear someone talking about a colleague's fabulous new job, and silently wish we could have *that* job; it sounds so much better than our own!

At times like these we have to stop and ask ourselves whether what we suddenly long for fits with the plan we have set for ourselves. These petty longings are not the same as dreams and hopes that are rooted in self-knowledge. If we examine them, we are sure to find that they have little or no meaning for our lives, even though they may fit another person's needs perfectly. We must always remind ourselves that no two paths to Oz are the same—and for good reason. Jealousy and envy are the wrong types of hopes and wishes and should always be avoided as they interfere with real growth.

Getting to Oz helps shield us from the annoyance of petty jealousy and envy. On the yellow brick road we know who we are as distinct from everyone else. We don't crave other people's experiences. We don't want their things or their spouses or their lives. We may admire them, but only for an instant. We only put a value on what we ourselves have earned and what we are capable of creating.

Are We There Yet?

By now you may have guessed that getting to Oz isn't really about arriving at a destination. The entire journey is the destination, as our progress in life is measured not by how far we have traveled but by how well we have lived. The way we construct our yellow brick road and how much it reflects our true purpose is the true measure of our success.

On our journey we have to ask ourselves these questions: Are we are putting in the effort required to live our lives well? Are we seizing life with both hands, learning to grow ourselves psychologically and spiritually? Are we learning all that we can about life's core truths—what it means to be an authentic person, to live an authentic existence, and to be fully human? If so, we are living life well. We are making good progress. The only standard we should adhere to is the standard we set for ourselves.

To live well means that we just don't hope to bump into awareness but that we vigorously go for it by making informed life choices. Whether it is building a career or a family or a relationship, we are put in each life situation to unfold ourselves psychologically and spiritually and to learn about what it means to be fully human. We use our good sense, our passion, and our courage to unfold the possibilities that are open to us in life.

Living well is a purposeful process. It requires that we learn every day from our successes and our failures. We can learn from the ordinary, everyday moments, but our peak experiences will yield the most wisdom. It is the things that require the most from us—the challenges we face on the road to Oz—that tell us the most about why we are here and what we have to do. These are the only measures of our progress in that they tell us how far we've come, and how much further we need to go. Any perceived emptiness in our status or achievement is a cause for us to re-evaluate—to question the road we're on and consider another course.

On the yellow brick road, we want to make every experience count for something. That is why bumps in the road are no cause for concern; they simply help us to re-program our inner GPS and start over again. Each new experience forms us and builds our character, molding and shaping us into the person we hope to become.

Choices and Consequences

I remember several years back when Jerry Springer thought about running for governor in the State of Minnesota. In the end, he dropped out of the race when, despite his political credentials, he failed to convince the voters that he was the right candidate for the job. In response to why he made this decision, Springer said: "I take responsibility for the choices that I have made in life. I should have known that becoming governor was not a possibility after doing *The Jerry Springer Show* for so many years."

Springer was alluding to the importance of being conscious on the journey. Our choices must lead purposefully to the goals we have set for ourselves. When we make choices that are deliberate and follow a line of intention, we will always get exactly where we need to be. Was Springer's true purpose in life to help people politically rather than on the air, or might he have fulfilled himself in either role? We don't know that answer, but one thing we do know: In life some experiences foreclose other experiences. We

43

take one path and forfeit another.

This is another way of saying that we get from life exactly what we put into it. When we begin the day with an *I don't care* attitude, we create an *I don't care* life, devoid of meaning or magic. We must have foresight into what we are trying to achieve at the end of the day. Are we trying to build material and public success alone? Or are we selecting life experiences that express our whole being—that is, who we are psychologically and spiritually? If our lives lack luster, perhaps it is because we have made choices without considering our true needs.

To live well means that we become the architects of our experience. This may sound hard and complicated, but really, it simplifies life greatly, in the moment and in the long run. With a blueprint for our lives, we select the experiences that support us and yield the greatest wisdom. The result: We don't have to suffer continuously to learn what is right for us; we know what we need and we go out and achieve it.

Yet no matter how accurate the blueprint, there will always be failures and missteps. The good news is everything counts—all experience is grist for the mill and fodder for our unique development. Jerry Springer did not run for governor but he learned something valuable: All things are *not* possible! To live well means that we use what we learn about ourselves to continue to grow. As we learn, we continually re-design the blueprint, and the learning curve shortens as we go.

A Trick of the Mind

Before entering the Emerald City, Dorothy and her companions put on green-colored glasses, then marvel at how green everything looks! It is easy to confuse ourselves in life, to trick ourselves into believing what is not so. But developing an authentic life is dependent upon our ability to see things clearly, including ourselves.

Most of us start out with a fairly distorted picture of who and what we are. We begin with an image in our mind based on feedback we receive from others. We have no accurate picture of who we are because this picture lies buried in the deepest part of ourselves, hidden from view until we are ready to perceive it. Often we follow the dictates of what is essentially a mistaken self-image for years. We continue to see ourselves in a certain light and assume that other people see us that way, too. Maybe they do, maybe they don't; the point is we never really know. Our friends and family usually tell us whatever version of the truth they think we want to hear. Because we do not see ourselves clearly, we tend to take paths that mislead us. We do our best to move through life, but frequently miss the mark when it comes to making important life decisions. If only we could see ourselves clearly! But we cannot—at least not yet.

Desperate for solutions, we seek them everywhere. Each new person that we meet and each new experience that we have becomes a potential route that could take us where we think we want to go. But these are just wild stabs in the dark; without knowing who we are, we have no idea what is good for us. The choices we make at this stage are based only on the most superficial understanding of our needs.

Eventually, we may get to the point of feeling worn out and discouraged. We may wonder if we will ever be able to fulfill our dreams. Despite our best efforts, we have failed to find our perfect partner, perfect job, or perfect life. This is not because we haven't tried hard enough; it is because our concept of what is perfect for us is very, very far from the truth. Our distorted self-image has thrown us off course. It is only when our lives begin to unravel that the truth is finally revealed to us. We begin to develop a clearer vision of who we are—and who we can become. No, it is not the picture of our dreams, but it is a true portrait that will guide us to an authentic life.

On the yellow brick road, a true image of who we are and who we can be begins to come clearly to mind. We know there is still much work to do, for we are creating our more authentic life as we go. But we are confident we will find our way because we have no illusions or misconceptions—only a realistic version of what is possible.

False Paths

Perception issues can also feed our fear and insecurity. The Scarecrow, the Tin Woodman, and the Lion all suffered from a flawed self-perception—totally failing to recognize their assets. It was only when their true potential began to unfold on the yellow brick road that they realized what was possible and stopped underestimating their strengths.

When we fail to perceive our strengths, we often find ourselves on a different kind of journey—not the intentionally paved road to Oz, but rather a hasty, unfocused path that takes us any old place. Without true thought or heart put into our journey, we take the quickest route possible to feeling good, which is rarely the wisest. Drugs, alcohol, food, and other easy fixes call out to us, especially when we feel weak or undervalued. When we choose this path, even though we have made these choices for ourselves, they only make us feel more powerless.

Some of us cling to the notion that if we could only get the one thing we are missing (a brain, a heart, courage) all would be well. But no quick fix can accomplish what takes time to build. No matter how we might wish to, we cannot reach Oz in a day. We need to take all the time we need—no more, no less—to get all that we can from our life experiences. Like archaeologists, we must refuse to leave our *dig site* until we have discovered exactly what we came for.

We may also fall into the trap of wanting more things—new homes, new lovers—a constant round of newness to fill up the emptiness. In perceiving newness as possibility, we may find out that what lured us to the next big thing was only a trick of the mind. This is a shame, as some of us will give up on promising relationships or jobs just because we are bored. Instead of mining them further, we will run off to the next opportunity, leaving a potentially valuable vein of gold behind.

Yet the yellow brick road to Oz offers rewards that are much deeper and longer lasting. One reward is the recognition of awesome gifts we can finally use. Another is the knowledge that happiness does not come from finding what is missing in our lives, but from learning to perceive what we have more clearly.

Life on the Road

As architects of our lives, from time to time we may need to pause to examine the structure we are creating. Where are we right now and what else might we need to do to finish our creation? If we're happy with what we see, we keep on going; if not, we may wish to modify the blueprint. Even this won't guarantee perfection, but it will increase our odds of ending up with something that reflects our true spirit and intention.

Once we are on the yellow brick road, we find it easier to build our lives. With a clear purpose and goal in mind, and a design for our future, we no longer say, "Maybe I'll continue moving in this direction." Instead we say, "I am heading in this direction because it is the right way for me." We get to Oz through careful plan and design.

Yet we're not afraid to take chances. We explore and test and stretch the limits, but we always do this with our best self. We don't shrink back from challenges, but we only fight the fights we believe in. We protect Dorothy from the Wicked Witch and chaperone her safely to Oz; we stand up to the flying monkeys and escape a field of sleep-inducing poppies through our sheer will and determination. By facing up to life's challenges, we create and live a life that reflects who we are and what we wish to become.

So we follow a blueprint, but allow for contingencies—the sudden jolts that take us in a direction we hadn't planned on, the unexpected changes of course. This is what good managers do. We prepare—which means we also anticipate change. We are never really lost on the yellow brick road. We can always use our authentic skills and talents to feel our way forward until we find the way that is right for us.

The life truly lived is a life that is always moving toward unfolding our true purpose. As we move forward, a pattern starts to emerge—a theme that reveals what our life is all about. We can see clearly where our mind and heart have led us thus far, and determine whether or not we have the courage to go the distance.

The key is to give life all we've got and never stop the search for our true self.

In the film *Gattaca,* there is a great scene in which Vincent, a genetic invalid, and his brother Anton, a genetic valid, set out to prove their superiority. The challenge is to see who can swim the farthest out to the sea. Vincent not only beats his genetically superior brother, but also saves him from drowning. When Anton asks his brother how he did it, Vincent replies, "I never saved anything for the swim back."

This is the ultimate lesson of the yellow brick road. We have to live our lives fully, no matter what disadvantages we start out with and who we have to battle along the way. We have the power to overcome adversity and take our place in the world in a deeply meaningful way. But we must give the yellow brick road all we've got—and not save anything for the trip back.

Chapter Four:

Packing Our Bags for Oz

We are ready to pack our bags for the journey to Oz. This trip is unlike any we've ever taken before, so we'll need a special set of navigational tools to help us take inspiration from the road and get where we want to go. On this trip what we leave out of our backpacks is just as important as what we put in them. As we set off on our journey, we may have to part with things that no longer serve us—people, ideas, and long-held beliefs that have carried us to this point in our lives. We know that anything or anyone important to our growth and wellbeing will meet up with us again in Oz.

And so, we take great pains to omit from our backpacks any items that weigh us down. This includes the worn-out ideas and rules that have been handed down to us but have little to do with our current needs, much less our hopes and dreams for the future. We particularly avoid taking along past troubles or emotional insecurities that obscure our way to Oz. These burdens only complicate our journey.

A Backpack Full of Potential

With our backpacks freed of the items we no longer need, we are ready to fill them up again with helpful items that bring about creative and constructive change to our lives. No longer enslaved by the rules and baggage that weighed us down, we have plenty of room for tools that help us navigate our journey. At this point these are *tools of possibility* because we have yet to discover their power and purpose.

The good news is, we don't have to search around to find these tools—they are already ours! Just like Dorothy's ruby slippers, they are waiting to be called into service and show us what they can do. These tools are nothing more or less than the basic instincts we have always possessed—but in Oz, we finally get to use them.

It has always been within our power to choose the best of what life has on offer to develop our authentic self. When we begin to use and trust in our tools of possibility we invest in our instinctive ability to self-examine and self-determine our lives.

Retrieving the Broomstick

We know what to take along in our backpacks. But before we sling them over our shoulder, we must ask ourselves if *we personally* have what it takes. Do we have the right spirit and attitude to make this journey? Are we prepared to approach our travels as if every moment on the road—good, bad, and neutral—contains insight for our lives? Are we ready to commit to a brighter future?

Part of Dorothy's great success was due to her positive attitude. When the Wizard asked her to retrieve the broomstick of the Wicked Witch of the West, she stepped right up to fulfill her duty. Ready and willing to meet her fate, whatever it might be, she headed straight for the witch's castle, taking the reins of her own life in her hands.

We all have this ability to rise to the occasion of our lives. We can all come to see our experiences as opportunity, using them to bring into the foreground of our awareness deeper meanings and hidden parts of ourselves. All we have to do is take up the same challenge the Wizard issued Dorothy: Retrieve the broomstick that is rightfully ours. We don't need a wizard to get us home; all we have to do is get on our very own broomstick and fly!

And so, forward we go to the yellow brick road with a backpack full of potential and a can-do spirit. This is our chance to allow our fantasies, dreams, and inner desires to point us in the direction of our true self. We trust that with every step, we will learn something about what we've lost, who we are, and who we can become.

The Tools of Possibility

Our first steps on the road to Oz are exciting ones, as we see the world through new eyes. No, the world hasn't changed, *we* have! There only appears to be an Emerald City up ahead of us, because our new way of seeing things has brought magic into our lives.

A vast treasure trove of experiences is ours for the taking! Now that we are free of our social selves and have no burdens to weigh us down, we are able to take inspiration from many sources. Whether seeing a film or a play, visiting a local museum or exploring the Louvre in Paris—whatever our budget allows—we absorb ideas that help us grow. A day at the beach or the mountains becomes more than just entertainment. Feasting on the ocean and the mountain peaks inspires us and fills us with awe.

Our hearts fill with joy as we linger over perspectives and meanings that we can apply to our own lives. Using our tools of possibility, we begin to draw a blueprint for the person we will become. These tools help us design, build, and follow a path of power and purpose that leads us all the way to Oz.

Tool #1: Psychological Awareness

In each of us there is a wizard of Oz, a psychologist, born with abilities of cognitive perception and understanding. As we develop these skills on the road to Oz, we find new perspectives and meaning in our relationship to all that surrounds us. We tap into the deepest parts of ourselves and crack the code of our authentic yearnings.

Imagine for a moment that we are cameras with the capacity to get an elongated, birds-eye view of each moment. All we have to do is position ourselves for a panoramic view. We relax physically and take a neutral, emotional, and mental stand on whatever is in front of us. Typically, we zoom in on our subject matter and then immediately stamp a label on it or decide on its meaning. Instead, we pull back a bit, opening ourselves up mentally and emotionally to take it all in.

The tool of psychological awareness allows us to approach each experience in Oz by taking the long view. We pay attention not just to what we observe, but how we process these observations— the ideas, images, and feelings that come up for us as a result of our interactions with life experience. When we take the long view of our lives, the psychological instrument inside of us kicks in.

With our new tool of psychological awareness, we find answers to a puzzle we gave up solving long ago. We get to meanings that the reasoning mind alone cannot understand, especially those that shed light on our past and present experiences. We *want* to know the truth of our lives and put effort into processing our experiences in ways that open up rather than shut down our response mechanisms. We begin to feel we are closer than ever to finding the way to our authentic selves.

But what if all of this openness is too much for us, exposing us to life in a way that causes anxiety or fear? Some of us start down the road to Oz after years of living behind a protective shield that we erected long ago. Perhaps we put it up in childhood, when we felt threatened or anxious. Or we may have tried to protect ourselves from the pain of facing a life challenge—our own suffering or that of a loved one. Sadly, we may have continued to live this way long after the threat has passed.

We learned to exist with defenses in place, avoiding pain of any kind. We somehow believed that it was better to deny than to know. But no matter how we defensively arranged not to think about something that troubled us, the thoughts and feelings did not go away. They remained inside us, causing mental and physical stress—the stress of unprocessed experience.

On the road to Oz, we escape from this self-imposed confinement and breathe the fresh air of truth. We work through our discomfort and, over time, gain psychological insight into whatever caused us to run from life. And the biggest bonus of all— we get a tremendous physical and emotional lift when we come to a psychological understanding that sets things right in our hearts and minds.

As we practice our awareness in the world, we slowly develop a relationship with our senses. This leads to the development of what we call a "sixth sense" in which we are able to intuit what is good for us in most, if not all, situations. Remember the Scarecrow's big dilemma at the crossroads? *Is it that way, or this way? Which way do I go?* With our new psychological awareness we no longer have to hazard a wild guess as to which path to take. Most often our sixth sense kicks in and helps us make good decisions, choosing the paths that lead to our authentic self.

Cracking the Code

In addition to helping us decipher our waking hours, the tool of psychological awareness helps us to unlock the meaning of our dreams. This is important, because dreams speak in a symbolic language, formed from our experience of the world. Dreams have much to tell us, revealing important information about our fears and yearnings. Remember my recurring dream about the chain-link fence? Finally understanding its message provided me with a better understanding of myself, and a gateway to my life's work. We can each be our own psychologists, using our skills of analysis to crack the code of our dreams.

The tool of psychological awareness opens up our ability to solve our lives. It is all there for us to see—ahead of us, behind us, around the next bend in the road, or as far back as we can go. We can read into our past, present, and future, providing a link to whatever vision we have for our lives.

Tool #2: Reclaiming the Lost Parts of Ourselves

What is it that calls us to Oz? What makes us want to risk everything, leaving our secure home base behind? For Dorothy, it was the threat of losing something very important to her—her dog Toto. For us it may be a similar challenge that asks us to rise up in ways we have never done before. Or perhaps we just wake up one morning different. We have a sense that there is something more for us in life, something we may have left behind long ago.

Tool #2 helps us to reclaim what we have lost. Like the Scarecrow's brain, the Tin Woodman's rusted heart, and the Lion's courage, the lost parts of ourselves are called back into service for the journey to Oz. We recover our inner magic, the skills and talents that have lain dormant because we have failed to use them. We move out into the world again, using all of the attributes that make us unique individuals. The minute we put our lost parts back into service we begin to get our real selves back.

What made us stop using the most valuable parts of ourselves—the special gifts that singled us out as individuals? Why did we abandon ourselves and let go of our dreams? It may be that our capabilities were unappreciated or were met with disapproval. Or, as in my own case, personal responsibilities may have interrupted our dreams-in-progress. Over time, these special gifts were shoved into the background of our awareness. Without our lost parts we were in limbo, waiting by the roadside for someone to come along and rescue us.

It turns out that *someone* is us. On the road to Oz, we choose once again to follow our own ideas and instincts. As free as the children we once were, we are brimming with delight at our ability to express ourselves without fear of criticism or ridicule or failure. Connecting with our lost ways of being rekindles a pure and honest expression of our value and purpose. It reminds us that we are more than just who we are today—we are the sum of all that has happened to us, past and present. Whatever we have lived, lost, and now recovered becomes grist for a vitally creative and individuated life.

In the classic children's book *Harold and the Purple Crayon*, Harold picks up a crayon and begins to draw himself into the world of his imagination. Finding the lost parts of our selves allows us to pick up the lost crayons of our vast and vivid imaginations and "draw" our lives the way we have always imagined them. As we design and follow the paths that enrich us most, it is as if we could actually see ourselves in the future, awaiting completion.

Perhaps it is necessary to lose ourselves before we can find our way again. Once our lost parts are restored, we begin to believe in the possibility of life's second acts. I've seen many individuals pick up the pieces of their lost lives and return to careers they left behind, or try something new that utilizes their reclaimed skills. I've seen doctors returning to culinary school, accountants taking up painting, and professional ballplayers heading to the classroom to teach—each trying to fulfill a long-ago vision they had of themselves. It is not so much that we go back to the beginning as

54

that we pick up where we left off.

Reclaiming the lost parts of ourselves is one of the great benefits of our journey to Oz. Now we are ready to leap over the gates of fate and gamble on our ability to stake out our own vision for what is possible. We can become the person we hoped to be.

In Transition

Here we go! Unlike Humpty Dumpty, we are put back together again. Excited by our new wholeness, we may be tempted to rush down the road to Oz. However, it pays to slow ourselves down, even hold back until we get comfortable in our new skin. After all, this may be the first time we have allowed ourselves to walk without a safety net, trusting our own resources and instincts. There are powerful forces at work in our environment, and not all of them are helpful to us. It takes time to learn who and what to trust as we make our way to Oz.

During this time we may choose to impose limits on ourselves—for example, how much time we spend with certain individuals who may not have been good for us in the past. We bring closure to our former lives and prepare for what lies ahead. We find that we begin to be comfortable saying "no"—a powerful word that many of us haven't used often enough. The difference is, now that we have so much good energy working for us, saying no becomes something positive, contributing to our sense of wholeness and wellbeing.

Reclaiming the lost parts of ourselves opens up doors we thought were closed to us forever. Like bringing old friends back into our lives again, it takes time to fully integrate these lost parts. We must be patient with this process, but once it is complete, there is no holding us back. Like Dorothy, we are ready to take the journey into a world we could only have imagined.

Tool #3: Self-Reliance

Dorothy's arrival in Oz was an exciting event. Throngs of townspeople cheered her because her house had fallen on the much-feared Wicked Witch of the East. A beautiful witch named Glinda came down from the sky to thank her. Was Dorothy a "good witch or a bad witch," Glinda asked. Bewildered, Dorothy responded that she was not a witch at all, just Dorothy from Kansas. She had no special powers that she knew of and only wanted to find her way back home. Glinda suggested the great Wizard of Oz might help her out, so Dorothy decided to make her way there. She set out for Oz with her dog Toto, wearing a pair of glittering slippers on her feet. Those slippers held great transformative powers, but it would be a while before she knew how to use them.

Like Dorothy, most of us do not believe in our own powers. We lack the self-confidence to bring our lives to the next level. In the very first steps we take on the road to Oz, we see the magic that can happen when we begin to rely on ourselves. Suddenly, people believe in us, perhaps even look up to us. It takes time to believe in our own magic, but on the road to Oz we soon learn that the only magic that occurs in our lives is the magic we create. We have to trust completely in ourselves to find our way. When we rely on our own instincts and trust our ability to follow through, we find our personal power when we need it most. The road to Oz does not disappoint us as long as we do not disappoint ourselves.

Some of us begin our journey to Oz with a head start: We have a mentor or teacher or friend who believes in us and gets us started down the road to our authentic selves. Glinda saw Dorothy's special powers and had confidence in her ability to find her own way. If we're lucky, we may have a Glinda in our own lives—someone who sees in us what we fail to see in ourselves. We may have parents, friends, or teachers who recognize our gifts and talents and encourage us to pursue them.

The best kind of help we can get is for others not to tell us what to do or pull strings for us, but to urge us to pick up the reins in our own lives. But although this kind of support and encouragement can start us down the road, it can't complete us. Eventually we have to take the journey to Oz for ourselves.

As Dorothy discovered, passivity in Oz will not do. On this journey we have to show what we are made of, and what we can do for ourselves. As we respond to each of the challenges that lie before us—doing our work in the world—we allow our talents to unfold. We find that the more we *do* the more we *become*. The more we rely on and celebrate our capabilities, the more we come to depend less on others and more on ourselves.

The tool of self-reliance is accessed not by wishful thinking or imagining, but via our own best efforts. We find that as we walk down the road to Oz using our new tool of psychological awareness we rely more and more on our own instinctual responses. Reclaiming the lost parts of ourselves has allowed us to take charge of our life path and self-determine what is best for us. Bravely, we begin to make our own magic in the world, and a bright future takes shape before our eyes.

The Very Best We Can Be

What does it mean to be "the very best we can be?" It means that we have gained the courage to rely on ourselves to produce good results in our lives. On the road to Oz we begin to trust that our own skills are good enough to carry us forward. We do not seek to be the best, but to be the very best we can be. We measure our progress not by some external standard but by how far we've come from where we were before.

We get to Oz by believing in our own personal power to bring about change in our lives. We begin by taking risks, crawling forward until we can walk, and then walking forward until we can run. We do not start off each day with doubt, but with affirmation. We set goals that remind us of what we are striving for. We get to Oz slowly but consciously, relying upon our own gifts and talents, and gaining the confidence to use them.

Tool #4: Self-Integration

Getting where we want to go in life requires that we make right choices that support our goals. When we reach a crossroads, it is usually because we have been presented with an opportunity. It is important that we choose wisely, as the development of an authentic life may depend on it. Yet, we can't decide. *Is it this way or that way?* We can reason our way to a solution (the Scarecrow's way) or we can feel our way forward (the Tin Woodman's way) or we can just tough it out (the Lion's way).

Tool #4, Self-integration, allows us to put together all that is available to us—our ability to think, feel, and act—to make right choices that reflect our true needs and capabilities. It helps that we now have the psychological awareness to be realistic about our possibilities, and the skills and self-reliance to achieve them. This in turn allows us to achieve a balanced state of mind so we can make right choices for our lives.

Before traveling the road to Oz we made decisions that failed to lead us to our desired goals. We felt certain the path we were on was the right one, and yet, like the Scarecrow, we somehow misread the signs. Perhaps we used our head instead of our heart, failing to acknowledge our true passion. Or swept up by a tidal wave of emotion, we failed to consider all the facts of a situation. Despite our best efforts, we lacked the balance and focus necessary to make choices that would support our hopes and dreams.

On the road to Oz we pull it all together—get all of our parts working as a team to promote our goals. We become present to our thoughts, and at the same time alerted to highly charged emotions that may cause us to act impulsively. We tune in to our feelings, at the same time looking for subtle cues and sensitivities that bring our true needs to light. We check in simultaneously with our thinking and feeling "channels" to arrive at what is true for our authentic selves.

It may help us to understand how we get so out of balance in the first place, and why it is so difficult for us to make decisions that support our goals. A look back reveals the root of our problems. Early on in our lives we tended to cover up our insecurities by simply guessing what to do instead of checking in with our thinking and feeling sides. When asked our opinion, we may have felt afraid or insecure, and simply blurted out a response to cover up what we didn't know. Over time, guesswork became a habit, and our authentic responses got lost altogether.

If we were fortunate, we were able to resolve these issues while we were still relatively young. If not, later on it became more difficult to take back the controls. Having constantly covered up for ourselves, we no longer knew what we thought or felt about anything! Yet we had to make decisions, so we took our cues from what others were doing or saying, hoping to adopt a strategy that would lead to some version of success. This practice only moved us further away from the possibility of authentic decision-making and further away from ourselves.

I know all about these challenges because I watched them play out in my own life, and once again, it was a recurring dream that helped me solve them. On the surface, the dream seemed obvious, but it took me time to fully comprehend what it meant. Like my dream of the chain-link fence, this dream had a powerful message for me, one that would play an important role in my own process of self-integration.

Walking on My Hands

In the dream I am walking on my hands for miles, occasionally tilting to the left, then right, but always returning to perfect center. I am keenly aware of what my whole being is doing in the moment. I have to be, or else I could not keep moving forward on my hands. People gather around me. I can see that they are trying to figure out how I do what I do. I just keep walking on my hands as if to show them that it is as natural as walking on two feet.

Over time, and through my own process of self-integration, the meaning of the dream became very clear. My intuitive self was telling me that the extraordinary is possible when we bring every part of ourselves into the here and now. The right amount of heart, mind, and courage gives us focus and balance, so we can assess the possibilities against the givens of our lives. Now we can walk on our hands or fly! This is how it feels when we get all of our parts working together as a team and what it means to create our lives with our own two hands.

Tool # 5: Patience

We have placed four of our tools of possibility into service and are beginning to make wise choices for living:

> We use our powers of awareness to develop psychologically and spiritually.

> We develop our natural gifts, increasing the choices that are available to us.

> We take charge of our lives, relying upon our instinctive responses.

> We put it all together, making right choices that reflect our true needs.

Our first steps on the road to Oz begin to bear fruit, and we enjoy a taste of what the future promises. *Yet, we are still not in Oz.*

The fifth and last tool in our backpacks is the one we may need to develop most of all. This is the tool of patience. It is what keeps us going, even when the terrain is treacherous and the road is steep. Few of us realize that patience takes practice. It is a learned skill, much like any other. It develops out of an appreciation for all that is on offer and an ability to understand its value in our lives. This appreciation plays an important role in our journey, buoying our spirits and causing us to feel better about ourselves. We look inside and see the inner light that shines there. We believe we can make it all the way to Oz, and we're okay with waiting as long as it takes to get there.

All in Good Time, My Pretty

Thanks to the tool of patience, we can take all the time we need to process our experiences, even those that might take longer than most. We can invest ourselves in new activities, without fear of wasting our time. And even if we are only halfway to Oz, we can take the time to celebrate what we have accomplished. In Oz, we make time our friend!

Before we made the journey to Oz, we were at the mercy of our schedules, moving from one activity to the next in nonstop pursuit of something we called "success." All of that changes on the road to Oz, with each of our tasks now assigned equal significance. We no longer think of time in terms of tradeoffs: If I put X amount of time into this activity, I only have X amount of time to put into that activity. We know all activities are equally important to our goals. This means we can focus exclusively on each thing we do, even to the point of losing ourselves to the "wow" of a moment—in effect, making time stand still.

Our patience pays off in amazing ways! It guarantees us quality time to complete our goals, releasing us from any fear or anxiety about the future. No longer a slave to the passage of time, we turn our hearts and minds to the spirit of each moment of each day, allowing ourselves exactly the amount of time we need to complete our journey.

No, we are still not in Oz. We have taken the road less traveled and, in the words of Robert Frost, "have miles to go before we sleep." But we keep on trying, day after day, making our way in the world. Patience leads to persistence. We doggedly go after our hopes and dreams and refuse to give up on ourselves. Giving up is what got us to a place of frustration and despair, and we don't want to go down that road again.

All That Glitters

In the film *Raiders of the Lost Ark*, archaeology professor Indiana Jones is summoned from his academic hiding place to save the Lost Ark of the Covenant from falling into the wrong hands. It turns out that the Nazis are in hot pursuit of the ark, which Hitler hopes will make his troops invincible. Of course, as anyone who has seen the film and its two sequels knows, the Lost Ark is a classic *MacGuffin,* a vehicle used to move the plot forward, its meaning never fully revealed. What the film is really about lies beneath the surface of the adventure: Indiana's growth as an

61

individual, as he overcomes shyness to take his place in the world. In later films, he resurrects his relationship with his father from whom he has been separated for years.

Our journey to Oz is a bold adventure, but it too has an important meaning that lies beneath the surface. In life, we may think in terms of finding success or glory or fame—the equivalent of a pot of gold at the end of the rainbow—but in the end, it is more about the experience than it is about any prize we might win at the end. That is why we have to bypass any surface offerings that glitter like gold and tempt us but will in the long run prove worthless to our cause.

We must always remember who we are and what we came for. We travel to Oz for the great adventure to our authentic selves and do only what is necessary to move our lives forward. The payoff comes not through any prize or breakthrough idea or experience, but through a succession of life's moments fully lived.

And what of that pot of gold at the end of the rainbow, the reward we hope to someday reach? That gold—or what we label "success"—is a *MacGuffin* just like the Lost Ark, meant to motivate us on our bold and fearless journey and bring us to our authentic selves. It has no other value. The real gold lies within, deep inside and glittering, as we move ever closer to Oz.

Chapter Five:
Twists, Turns, and Tornadoes

It's great when life is going well, but as we all know, adversity strikes when we least expect it. How we handle ourselves when meeting one of life's challenges says a lot about how far we've traveled down the road to Oz. When we meet our disappointments with an eye toward growth and self-improvement, our life opens to us in meaningful ways.

The idea of meeting a challenge makes it sound as if these are practical problems with straightforward solutions, but that is far from the truth. There is nothing simple or straightforward about divorce, illness, or the death of a loved one. There is nothing status quo about failing an important exam or losing a job we've held for years. The goal is to face our difficulties squarely as Dorothy did— meeting the tornado head on with all the spirit and determination we can muster. The awesome power of such events often brings our lives clearly into focus, inspiring a fighting spirit—a survival instinct we did not know we possessed.

On the road to Oz everything changes. We meet many tests of our endurance, but we learn to use them to our advantage, each time learning some new piece of information that gives us the confidence to get back on the road and complete our journey. We learn new ways to tune in to our hearts and minds, and as a result we become resilient, hardy individuals. We may not be able to prevent the tornado from coming, but at least we will have the skills and knowledge to lessen its impact by turning twists and turns into triumphs.

Opening the Gates

On the yellow brick road, we learn how to prepare for life's confrontational and pivotal moments by looking at areas of our lives that need to be changed. Most challenges seem to arrive in our lives as bolts from the blue. Yet, if we look back, we may be able to see that there were signs.

In the stage play and film *West Side Story*, the song "Something's Coming" refers to the feeling we get deep in our bones when something major is about to happen in our lives. What we do with this feeling can make all the difference in the way things turn out. By tuning in to our hearts and minds we can better prepare ourselves for change before it is thrust upon us. If we can get our hearts and minds engaged in the *process* of change, we may be able to use it to our advantage.

We know that if we don't shake ourselves out of the rut we're in, something is bound to come along and hit us hard. In truth, the call for change is rising from within. We have to open the floodgates and release the pent-up energy that is threatening to burst forth and reappear in some external form—a monster tornado that knocks us off our feet. Releasing the pressure that has been building inside us helps us let go of whatever it is we have been holding onto. Likely it is something that no longer has value in our lives. Opening the floodgates not only gives us access to internal resources, it allows new information and experiences to flow through us and get us moving again.

When we don't tune in to the need for change in our life, it is likely that the knocks we receive will be much greater than they might have been. They will have to be to force us out of our rut and back on the road to Oz. They may come in the form of severe health issues or broken relationships or a loss of job or assets. Even though every life experience contains a valuable lesson, these harder knocks can be tough to bear and are worth trying to minimize or prevent. By tuning in to change when it is needed, we may avoid these harder knocks.

How do we know when it is time? Perhaps we are in a job or relationship that is no longer getting the best from us or causing us to grow. Or we may have less energy and feel drained by our daily routines. If we have learned everything we can from this part of our journey, it is time to open the gates. We may not keep the tornado from coming, but at least we will meet it on our own terms. If it knocks us down, we will find a way to get up again and grow from the experience. On the road to Oz, we continually reboot our lives in this way, getting stronger with every challenge we face.

The Road to Hardiness

How do we become resilient, hardy individuals, ready to handle whatever life throws at us? How do we prepare ourselves to meet the oncoming tornado so that we are ready whenever and wherever it strikes? We cannot prevent some hardships from occurring, but we can shore up our ability to meet life's challenges. It was Hamlet who said: ". . . if it be not now, yet it will come—the readiness is all." This readiness for whatever life has in store for us is what we refer to as "hardiness." It is the very best defense we can put up against life's hard times.

The Hardiness Attitudes

Hardiness begins with three powerful attitudes. These attitudes help us to approach life's challenges as valuable lessons offering opportunities for learning and growth. The twists and turns of our lives will occur whether or not we are ready for them—but if we are prepared, we can work through life's challenges more readily and use them to our benefit. The following three Hardiness Attitudes help stabilize our position on the road to Oz:

The Attitude of Commitment

We bring our full attention to working through life's setbacks. We know that every bump in the road is worth our imagination and effort. We may feel the urge to run, but we do everything in our power to face up to our challenges. That's because we know that withdrawing from painful circumstances won't make it any easier the next time we are challenged. We hang tough, meet our problems, and dedicate ourselves to ways of solving them. *We keep digging until we find a solution to our problems.*

The Attitude of Control

We do not operate passively in our lives but try to find positive ways of getting unstuck. We do not let ourselves sink into powerlessness but find gateways of release that allow us to move on in our journey. We dig inside for skills and resources to solve the problems we face. If we don't possess the skills we need to find our way out of our current trials, we continue the journey, gathering skills and knowledge along the way. *We take charge of the problem, using our skills and talents.*

The Attitude of Challenge

We see every one of life's twists, turns, and tornadoes as beneficial. We recognize that no matter how difficult the challenge we are facing, it may open up new, fulfilling pathways for living. The idea is to face up to stressful events, trying our best to understand them, learn from them, and solve them. *No matter what we face, we remain optimistic about our future.*

The three Hardiness Attitudes encourage us to look more carefully at the path we're on. Even if it seemed as if our life was going along well, whatever has happened in our life is now cause for concern. We are being asked to dig a little deeper and consider new possibilities. We may need to make some major adjustment or minor repair to a job or relationship. Or, we may need to change course entirely. The Hardiness Attitudes force us to take whatever action is necessary on this leg of the journey.

Putting Things in Perspective

The Hardiness Attitudes give us the courage and motivation to see the situation before us in a new light. With less fear, anxiety, and hesitation, we can now take the next step—using the Hardiness Perspective Questions to enter into a thought process that takes us toward a solution. These questions may seem simple on the surface, but I have seen them work time and again to get individuals unstuck and moving again. Each question explains a new perspective or way of looking at a problem. The questions should be answered as they apply to the current situation, but may be used each time we face a new challenge on the road to Oz.

The Hardiness Perspective Questions

Regarding the current difficulty, would you say that it is common to many people?

This question helps us see that what is happening to us could happen to anyone! It's not that we're cursed or that life has it in for us. All we need is a new tool to help us dig our way out of our current fix and we will be on our way. Shifting to the *commonplace perspective* allows us to see things as they really are and keep negative emotions in check. We are free to solve the problem and continue our journey to Oz.

Realistically, would you say that this situation is manageable?

This question allows us to see the stressful things that are happening to us for what they are—neither the end of the world nor the best thing that ever happened to us. By applying the *manageability perspective* to our problem, we inject a healthy dose of realism and allow ourselves to slip into neutral. By slowing ourselves down, we figure a way to solve whatever trouble we are in.

Would you say that you could improve upon what is happening?

This question lets us decide whether the situation can be improved with our effort. If we acknowledge that there are avenues of improvement open to us, then we no longer view the situation as hopeless. The *improvement perspective* encourages us to accept that we have a role and a responsibility for making things better. We take the reins in solving our own difficulties.

How long do you feel it will take to work through this problem?

This question helps us determine how much time we have available to us to deal with whatever trouble we are in. The *timeframe perspective* makes it easier for us to manage our expectations and emotions by giving us a sense of how long it will take us to work through the problem. Without this perspective, our minds may chart a course for forever, and we may give up before we start.

How do you know that any of your efforts will get you unstuck?

This question prepares us for outcomes that are beyond our control. No matter how hard we try, we will never be able to forecast every event on the road to Oz. The *unpredictability perspective* lets us see that even if we are well prepared, some life circumstances can take us by surprise. The best strategy in preparing for such events is to expect the unexpected.

On the road to Oz, our goal should never be to escape our challenges, but like Dorothy, face up to them, using whatever tricks and tools we have learned along the way. The Hardiness skills help us not only face our hardships but use them to our advantage. Susan's story illustrates the Hardiness Attitudes and Perspectives in action.

Susan's Story

When Susan first came to see me she was despondent. After fifteen years as an actress, she suddenly found herself struggling to succeed. Although she had never made it as a bona fide star, Susan had always been successful in landing small TV roles and the occasional stage play. But now that reality TV had taken hold, there were fewer roles for people with her experience. She felt more and more defeated as she saw her career slipping away.

Using the Hardiness Attitudes, I helped Susan to understand the level of attention that was required to solve her problems. Once she was committed to finding a solution, the Hardiness Perspective

Questions helped her focus on the source of her troubles. The *commonplace perspective* helped her understand that bumps in the road happen to everyone, not just her. She let go of her anger, which freed her to use the *management perspective* to explore new avenues of work and the *timeframe perspective* to develop a realistic amount of time to meet her new goals.

Today, Susan has moved on with her life. She continues to work as an actress, but has found enjoyment in her new career—evaluating scripts for a major talent agency. By searching both inside herself and outside in the world for solutions, she gained an understanding of her problems. Most important, Susan now has the Hardiness skills she needs to handle and make the most of life's challenges.

From Seeing to Solving

Most of our setbacks on the way to realizing our true selves arise from deep within. It is only after gaining deeper insight into ourselves that we know where to start digging for solutions. At last we understand the source of the influences that have temporarily stalled our efforts. But how do we go from *seeing* to *solving*? Just ask the Scarecrow, the Tin Woodman, and the Lion! Each had to learn that it is rarely a lack of talent or imagination that prevents us from fulfilling our true potential—it is our insecurities, fears, and emotional baggage.

To help my patients go from seeing to solving, I've developed a set of tools I call *The Five Useful Forms of Self-Understanding.* I have found these to be helpful in rooting out the cause of deep personal issues, especially those brought on by insecurity, anxiety, and fear. When we establish a line of inquiry into ourselves, we learn to let go of outmoded behaviors that are threatening to derail us. These tools will help us anytime we are stalled out on the road to Oz.

The Five Useful Forms of Self-Understanding

#1 Personal Limitations

Personal limitations can keep us from getting what we want out of life. The more we avoid these limitations, the more powerful the twists, turns, and tornadoes become. Instead, we must not avoid them, but find a way to work through them. For example, an aspiring dancer with performance anxiety must figure a way around this issue. Or, someone who does poorly on exams must come up with an alternative route to medical school. To pursue our dreams, we have to develop beyond whatever personal limitation is preventing us from moving forward. *We can get beyond whatever is holding us back.*

#2 Misunderstandings

New experiences on the road to Oz open us to a range of people and situations. This is both good news and bad news. The good news is, we learn much from our experiences and develop as individuals. The bad news is, all of these new relationships may result in personal misunderstandings. We have to look at these as learning vehicles that smooth the road ahead and take us more quickly to our true selves. *The solutions almost always lie within.*

#3 Clashes of Will

We are not alone on the road to Oz. There are others along on the journey, and some of them may refuse to share the road. Fortunately, the road to our authentic selves is humanizing. It forces us to appreciate the differences between ourselves and other individuals, and to recognize that each of us has a right to thrive. We can realize our own potential while allowing others to realize theirs. Alfred Adler identified this spirit as "healthy competition." The authentic person can compete and thrive without destroying others in the process. *There is plenty of room on the road.*

#4 Victimization

Sadly, no matter what attitude we bring to the journey, some of us may encounter brutal treatment by others on the road to Oz. This can happen in our professional or personal lives and may take the form of physical or mental abuse, or being bullied or harmed in some other way. Becoming a victim of such abuse does not have to destroy us. If we understand what is happening, we can mobilize ourselves to authentic spirit and action. Taking decisive action prevents us from being victims. *We can rise up from powerlessness and become our best selves.*

#5 External Forces

Sometimes we find ourselves in negative situations that have been triggered by factors beyond our control. We live in a climate of ever-shifting social, economic, and political forces. We have to learn how to adapt to changes in our environment and make these forces our friends. We can use external forces to our benefit instead of allowing them to defeat us. *We can manage the world on our own terms.*

Good Faith, Bad Faith

Sometimes we just want someone to make it all go away—the confusion, the pain, the suffering. Who hasn't gone through hard times and wished for a savior? These are the times when we feel powerless to change what is happening to us. We're in freefall, and the loss of control can be frightening. I know this from my own experience and from speaking with so many individuals in crisis. I know, too, that even in life's most challenging times, the ability to move forward is always within our own power. There is always an escape route; we just have to choose it.

Unfortunately, some of us deny ourselves access to this power. We deceive ourselves about our right to freely choose who we are and how we want to live. I call this *bad faith*—a lie that we tell ourselves about the extent of our freedom over life circumstances.

71

Bad faith is what causes us to put little effort into battling our way back from our setbacks. When the tornado comes through we just let it happen and fail to get out of the way. We allow ourselves to get knocked off the path to Oz.

When we act in bad faith over a long period of time, it becomes harder each day to see the possibilities of starting over. Imagine a prison cell in which we are locked up, away from the world. Years go by, and one day we realize the door to our cell has always been open but we weren't observant enough to notice it. We realize that we are free to go. Instead, we back away from the door, letting our freedom slip away. Why? Because we see how we have failed to make a choice that would have assured us our freedom. To punish ourselves, we remain in the cell, denying ourselves the right to make this choice.

Good faith allows us to operate differently in the world. When we are of good faith, we believe we have the right to self-determine. We carve out possibilities, no matter how many detours come our way. Some of us even learn to thrive on setbacks, using them as springboards for opportunity and the route to a better life. We not only get back on the road to Oz, we take joy in each leg of our journey, living out each new detour as a possibility. By doing this, we make an investment in ourselves. Unfortunately, as the following story illustrates, not all of us make this choice.

Mark's Story

Mark was in his midfifties when the tornado hit. It was a time in life when many of us are just beginning to enjoy the fruits of our labors. He seemed to have it all: a beautiful and devoted wife, two loving children, and an excellent career as a computer engineer. But despite Mark's numerous achievements and seeming comfort with his life, over time Mark had built up a dependency on alcohol and prescription drugs. Things had gotten so bad that recently his wife had threatened to leave him. Mark did not believe that would ever happen.

Then came the tornado. After thirty years of marriage, Mark's wife Sara told him she wanted a divorce. Mark went into a tailspin.

72

Sara had been the one thing in his life he could count on. He had always been devoted to her, telling more than one person that she was responsible for his happiness and success. What few people knew was how much Mark's sense of self depended upon Sara. Without her, he could conceive of no life at all. Instead of using good faith to embark upon a recovery plan, Mark saw himself as a victim of events. He could not develop a perspective that would allow him to mourn his loss and then pick up the pieces of his life and move on.

Mark went into a downward spiral. For the next ten years, he walked through his life as a ghost. He could find nothing to dissuade him from thinking his life was over. He would get up in the morning and go through the motions of living but, in fact, his life was at a complete standstill, as will often happen when one chooses bad faith over good. His acceptance of the utter futility of his existence finally led him to the worst bad faith choice of all: the choice to take his life. Fortunately, a friend brought him to the hospital in time to save him, and Mark received the support and care he needed to get well.

What Mark failed to comprehend is that we only stop being victims of external events in our lives when we acknowledge the free choice that is ours to make. This means that no matter what befalls us, how beaten down we get, we must never forget that we have the power to choose something different for ourselves, even if it is only a different perspective on what has happened. This shift in perspective may be all we need to rescue us from hard times and bring us back to the land of the living.

I Saw the Angel

Beneath my photo on Facebook there is a quote by Michelangelo: "I saw the Angel in the marble and carved until I set her free." This epitomizes what I believe to be my deep commitment to acting in life out of good faith. The idea that we can carve out our futures even under the most difficult circumstances has saved me more than once, always moving me to higher ground. Everyone is capable of operating out of good faith;

we just have to choose it.

On the road to Oz, we are all Michelangelos, carving ourselves into great works of art, using our imagination, reason, and will. We have a vague idea of who we might one day become, but it is exciting to watch each feature emerge from that lump of clay! When we take a risk and leave Kansas for the wide world of experience, we take the first bold steps toward creating the lives we imagine.

The road to Oz is our very own block of marble, ready and waiting for us to make it our own. "Come," says the road, "I am yours. Travel me, carve me into whatever shape you wish." When we say yes to the road, we become experience artists, traveling a path to our authentic selves.

Owning the Road

On the road to Oz setbacks are as important as triumphs. Twists, turns, and tornadoes are the inspiration for our journey, fueling our inner fire and bringing our wildest imaginings to life. The challenges we face on the road to Oz are signals that it is time to take a leap forward, to be daring and inventive and free. When we tune in to these signals, we *own the road.*

Of course, the hardest knocks can be difficult to take, but thankfully, they don't come often. The Wicked Witch of the West isn't waiting for us around every corner. But when we are ready for the next big stage of our development, she will likely appear, challenging us to take that next bold leap into the future. These are the times when we tend to feel the most hopeless, frightened, and alone. We must remember the process and believe we have the reason, passion, and courage to find the way forward.

Life's twists and turns can only harm us if we fail to use them as gateways to the future. When we meet life's greatest challenges, we must wonder what we are meant to learn from them—what is the hidden opportunity? Think of it as drawing a Chance card in the game Monopoly. The cards aren't always positive, but what chance are we being given? We must think of it as a gift that will bring us to the next critical stage of development.

Meanwhile, we walk forward, led by a bold personal vision of the future. Present to possibility, we don't let twists and turns set us back; instead, with our imagination lighting the way, we are drawn toward our goals, purpose, and ideals. All of this requires a conscious effort on our part, an active participation in our own lives.

Dreaming Our Way to Oz

Dorothy is our role model for this active mode of living. She dares to dream the boldest dream imaginable—to see what lies over the rainbow, not as an escape, but as a solution to her problems. The opposite of the active mode is the reactive mode. We are in reactive mode when we let life's difficulties overwhelm us and feel there is nothing we can do to bring about a change in our lives. Unlike Dorothy, we act only in response to events and are unable to move forward.

When we live our life in reactive mode, we have no dream, no vision of the future to carry us forward. We sleepwalk through life, assuming everything good that can happen to us has already happened. This fatalistic viewpoint negates our having to take responsibility for making bad decisions. But it also sidesteps our ability to make good decisions that would get us to Oz.

But let's go back to Dorothy's dream. Clearly, we are meant to see Oz as the vivid workings of Dorothy's imagination—an effort to sort through a difficult situation. In her dream state, the mean Miss Gulch became an evil witch, and Professor Marvel became a Wonderful Wizard. Her new friends—the Scarecrow, the Tin Woodman, and the Lion—bear a striking resemblance to her old friends back home. But if Oz is just a figment of Dorothy's vivid imagination, why did it succeed in bringing her spirit back to life? And how, in our own times of trouble, can we manage to do the same?

For the answer to this question, we have to go all the way back to the sixth century and the Mayan civilization. The Mayans believed that we dream ourselves into being through the imaginings of our hearts and minds. When there is nothing left to learn and we have *exhausted the dream*, we begin again, imagining a new vision of ourselves and dreaming it into being. According to the Mayans, we keep moving forward in this way, creating and living out our dreams, growing and changing and evolving.

When we journey to our own dream of Oz, we agree to go wherever the dream takes us—and the next dream and the next—through each twist and turn in the road, understanding that the process is more important than the result. We let the imaginings of our hearts and minds come true through the actions we take. We recognize that we alone are responsible for the process of dreaming ourselves into being.

What our dreams represent is possibility. They encourage us to see life's challenges as invitations to the awe and mystery of life. When we can suffer and still find ourselves attached to the beauty of life, we realize the possibilities inherent in all adversity. When we manage to stay on the road to Oz, we get to the other side of our suffering and remain positive about what life has yet to offer us. In this state of being, beyond any sense of victimhood or retribution, even our brokenness is something beautiful to behold.

Tom's Story

I met Tom at a pivotal time in his life. A high-ranking fireman, Tom loved his job, but lately something was tugging at him—a new dream for his life. Tom was an idea person, always coming up with ideas he failed to put into practice. Now, he had an idea for a product—education dolls for teaching fire rules to kids. He thought this idea was good enough to pursue but was afraid to move away from his "real career" and from a path that had been good to him. He wondered whether to pursue or abandon his dream.

The first therapist Tom went to see advised him to put his dream on hold and try to be happy with what he had already achieved in life. "Not everyone," the therapist advised him, "is meant to fulfill his dream." I disagreed and told Tom that as long as his dream was realistic—and it certainly was, in light of his track record and experience—he needed to trust it. I helped him see why unfolding our true purpose is what keeps us alive.

Tom's story shows how life's pivotal moments don't always come in the form of some disaster. Nothing was particularly wrong in Tom's life, except that he felt unmotivated and uninspired. He was lucky to recognize this as a problem, as so many of us do not.

Challenge and Choice

Years after being incarcerated in a concentration camp, the great writer and philosopher Viktor Frankl penned his seminal work, *Man's Search for Meaning*. His magnificent words have inspired countless individuals, myself among them. Frankl wrote: "Everything can be taken from a man but one thing: the last of the human freedoms—to choose one's attitude in any given set of circumstances, to choose one's own way."

The idea that no matter what happens to us in life, we have the freedom to choose our way is what has kept me on my own personal and professional mission to Oz. Each time some unexpected event or situation has threatened to pull me off course, I used this idea to navigate my way back to my goals and, if necessary, to choose a new life direction. Over time, I came to see that each challenge I faced brought about some needed change in my life. It was gratifying to know that I alone had been the instrument of these changes.

To self-determine our existence means that we always have the right to choose the road we take in any situation. It may be a difficult situation, but we get to choose how we perceive it and what we take away from the experience. No matter how dire things are, knowing that we can choose a new path helps us to feel alive again so that we can get back on the road to Oz.

When we make a choice for ourselves we are in active mode, seeking a way into the problem instead of a way out. The silver lining will come—but first we have to make the choice to move in some positive direction. By seeing hope where we saw none, we alone determine the spirit of who we are to become and how. Again, in the inspiring words of Viktor Frankl: "When we are no longer able to change a situation, we are challenged to change ourselves."

Out of the Darkness

It may seem daunting to rise up out of our darkest moments and begin again in order to find new dreams to sustain us. But life always has something new to offer us, and sometimes we have to bring ourselves out of the depths of despair to find it. Building a new dream requires just as much grit, determination, and intention as it did to fight the last battle we faced, and sometimes we just don't feel we have the energy or desire to start over. Didn't we try our hardest last time, and look what happened. But on the road to Oz, looking back is not an option. There is no way to go but forward.

So onward to Oz we go, through the stirrings of our hearts and minds. As long as we are fully engaged and alive, and have a new dream to guide our lives forward, we can rise to any challenge. There is somewhere we are longing to be—over the rainbow—that our dreams are helping us to create. As we follow the road, unfolding our purpose, we are in the active mode of becoming. We live in process, in the space between where we came from and where we are going, adapting and changing and growing with each twist and turn in the road.

Chapter Six:
Signs, Symbols, and Sorcery

Now that we are on the road to Oz, we are excited by the possibilities, open to learning all that we need to know to expand into our authentic self. Some of these possibilities are readily apparent, and we use our new awareness to read the signs that are right in front of us, pointing our way to a brighter future. But some gateways to the future are still closed off to us. To walk through these closed doors, we have to become skilled detectives, using our new psychological awareness to burrow deep into ourselves.

The past holds important clues, helping us to understand why we did the things we did. In the past, we may have ignored opportunities, missing signs or clues that might have brought us closer to fulfillment. No longer! On the road to Oz we become skilled sign-readers. We learn to decode and demystify the signs and symbols from the past that provide a direction and purpose for the future. The future won't just walk up and tap us on the shoulder; we have to reach out and claim it as uniquely ours.

We may have to dig down deep to make sense of things, working in the dark to shed light on issues that have haunted us for years and prevented future growth. No, we don't just get handed the keys to the city like Dorothy did, and we don't have the ruby slippers to guide us forward. But we do have one big advantage: We are on the yellow brick road where past, present, and future are melded together. Here, it is easier to know what to look for; our newfound awareness opens our eyes as never before.

Hunting for Clues in the Past

To begin, let's imagine a tree—a big, strong oak—and then think of how that oak began as a tiny seedling, planted in the earth. Wherever it was planted, the earth became the foundation for its life, the basis for its growth and development. Regardless of how our lives started out, the nurturing and support are now up to us. We can even re-seed the past, depositing fresh, multi-layered soil, to grow into the individuals we want and need to become.

As we look around, the past may overwhelm or surprise us, especially since our new awareness tends to heighten everything we see. Viewing the past from the road to Oz is like experiencing a 3D movie for the first time and being startled by its stark reality. In a 3D movie, things pop out of the screen at us, and we feel that we are truly there—that we can reach out and touch the characters just as we would if they were standing right before us. From our vantage point on the road to Oz, this is how our new awareness allows us to see the past. It can be a transforming experience!

With our new perspective, we can reinterpret and reframe events that happened long ago. We can take a virtual walk around ourselves—a hologram frozen in time—circling and circling it until we are able to see the whole of anything that had previously occurred. This is absolutely critical to our self-development. We not only see the entire truth of a situation, we see what triggered our responses and caused us to act in certain ways. We know what we did and why we did it.

This is important, because to a large extent, who we are in the present is largely determined by our view of ourselves in the past. The past exists only because we give it meaning. Whether or not our past inhibits, harms, or liberates us has everything to do with what we *believe* to be true. That is why it is so important to reframe our ideas of ourselves, based not only upon who we are today, but who we wish to be.

On the road to Oz we learn that it is up to us how we see things. That doesn't mean we should ever lie to ourselves. We are merely re-interpreting the past, not by altering the facts in any way, but by using the wisdom that comes from growth and maturity to bring ourselves understandings that did not exist before. Our ability to understand the truth about ourselves was always there; but now, on the road to Oz, our new awareness and openness enables us to make use of it.

The Case of the Lost Self

Agatha Christie's fictional detective Hercule Poirot was known for his ability to solve cases from a psychological perspective. Rather than searching crime scenes, Poirot focused more on the nature of the victim and the psychology of the murderer. He probed and interrogated his suspects until he arrived at a solution to the crime. In the search for our authentic selves, we have to operate like Poirot, using our psychological tools to understand ourselves better and bring back the part of us that has been lost.

Like a good detective, we start out by asking many questions. Using the insight and understanding we have gained on the yellow brick road, we burrow deep into our psyches and hunt around in the stories of our past. Then we step back and look at ourselves from a distance. *Hmmm . . . What do we have here?* Like Poirot, we try to solve the mystery, piecing together the puzzle of our past. Gradually, we shed new light on our self *then,* our self *now*, and finally, the self we wish to become.

Many of our self-questions begin with the word "why." "Why did we take that job over the other one offered?" or "Why did we fall in love with that particular person?" As we study our answers to each *why* question, we may begin to see a pattern emerging, a pattern that may explain our motivation for doing certain things in certain ways. This is a sign we need to pay attention to, as patterns often are.

We go deeper. We notice that in the past our standard mode of behavior, our *operating pattern*, was at least to some extent predictable. Perhaps there was a theme to our behavior that we can only identify now in hindsight. We may have had a tendency to take the path of least resistance or the path of pain. Or, we may have made choices based on parental expectation, sacrificing our own needs.

Whatever we did in the past, *it is time to change things up!* We can now start to think about making choices that are more aligned with what we want for the future. If, for example, we have always chosen the easy road, the next time we have an important decision to make we can choose to challenge ourselves. Or, if we have tended to make choices based upon parental approval or expectation, next time we might make a point of asking ourselves "What is it that *I* want?" Seeing the patterns of the past helps us choose a more authentic way of expressing ourselves now and in the future. This opens up pathways that up until now have been closed to us. We begin to see ourselves as agents of change.

Patients often ask me why they have so much trouble letting go of the past. They want to know why they keep hanging on to past hurt, resentment, and regret, and repeating the same mistakes. My response is always the same: "You have to change yourself to change the past." When we change ourselves we can move away from the past that shaped but does not own us. We can dig deeper for solutions and new perspectives. Instead of suffering with past memories and hurts, we can use them as clues to our psyches and as stepping stones to growth and change.

Dorothy's Perspective

To help us understand the psychological perspective we bring to our past choices, let's take a look at the choices Dorothy made before she arrived in Oz. If Dorothy were to hunt for clues in the past, what questions might she ask herself about the choices that she made? Here are some things she might want to know (and maybe we do, too!):

Question #1: Why did I run away from home when I knew a tornado was approaching?

Question #2: Why didn't I stand up for myself against the mean Miss Gulch?

Question #3: Why did I decide to run back home after meeting Professor Marvel?

Let's assume Dorothy is asking herself these questions from her vantage point on the yellow brick road to Oz. Now, far from home, she has gained the perspective and insight she needs to understand things she could not possibly have understood before. *She has changed herself to change the past.* As a result, she arrives at the following answers to these questions—answers that reflect her new psychological awareness and shed light upon the choices she will begin to make from now on.

Answer #1: I failed to think things through and acted impulsively.

Answer #2: I didn't know my own power.

Answer #3: I was afraid to follow through on my dreams.

The Q and A method works equally well when applied to our own lives, helping us better understand choices we made in the past. Now we can change our view of the past without changing what actually happened. We are neither wizards nor witches—yet we are able to perform magic, as we begin to see the past in a whole new light. Suddenly, we understand the person we once were, appreciate the person we have become, and realize the steps we need to take to become fully authentic individuals. We see past, present, and future—all together!

Pam's Story

Pam, a vibrant and intelligent thirty-two–year–old research chemist, came to see me with a problem that is not uncommon. Although she loved her career, she suddenly felt stuck in her life, a victim of the choices she had made. All Pam's friends were now married and having children. Yet when Pam really thought about it, she wasn't sure this path was right for her. It wasn't that she was unhappy with her choices; it was that she was in mourning for a past she could not change and in fear of a future she could not yet see.

Five years earlier, despite the fact that her friends were all taking different paths, Pam had returned to school to pursue her dream of becoming a research chemist. To fulfill her dream, she had ignored the social pressure to get married and start a family.

Instead, she had struggled along for years with very little money and no personal life. She had sacrificed the path of least resistance in favor of a path of purpose and dedication. Pam's depression had come on suddenly, fueled by the sense that she had missed something in her life that she could never get back. She began to see her life in terms of lost years and felt a very real fear that the choices she had made might not have been right for her after all.

To help Pam get back on track, I explained to her that although she could not change the past, she could change her view of it. Over several months, we worked on getting her to see herself as I saw her—a courageous and unique individual who had endured years of sacrifice to have what was most important to her. Her past showed all the signs of a person who had been driven by a desire for learning, self-development, and spiritual growth. Pam came to understand that these choices had been deliberate and had gotten her where she was today. No, she could not change the past, but she could celebrate the person she had become and plant new seeds for the future based on her real desires.

It is vitally important when looking back at our lives that we not only look at our choices but affirm them—yes, even those that led us temporarily astray. Remember, there are no wrong turns in life; we are exactly where we need to be right now. We have only to see ourselves as we really are, and then begin the re-seeding process for the future.

The Timeline of Our Lives

Before we start down the yellow brick road, we are mainly aware of ourselves in the moment. We fail to understand why we have made certain choices and even wish we could take them back. We have a fairly limited view of our lives and fail to take in the whole of a great chain that forms our existence, from the beginning to where we are right now. Our limited view prevents us from seeing that certain steps were critical to our development. Now, through the lens of maturity, we have the opportunity to step back and view our lives as a whole. When we take the long view of our lives and stop focusing exclusively on the moments, signs and patterns begin to emerge that offer clues to our future.

We can make hunting in the past for clues easier by constructing a life timeline. It's a simple exercise that reveals a great deal about our patterns and choices. Here's how it's done:

> We begin by drawing a horizontal line on a blank page. Mark off each decade of life up until the present—for example, at age 50, there are five equal sections of the timeline. For each decade, fill in the pertinent social events of the time—for example, depending upon when the timeline begins: The Kennedy Assassination, 9/11, the war in Iraq, Hurricane Katrina. Finally, enter significant life events—graduation, first job, marriage, divorce, etc. We include the triumphs as well as the challenges— any occurrence that may have had a profound effect upon our development.

When we're done with our life timeline we have a complete record of our lives up until the present—not just dots on a line, but single events that made up the whole of our lives. This helps us begin to see life as a continuum and moves us away from a tendency to focus too much on just one occurrence or perceived mistake. We understand our lives in process and notice our potential for change.

Now let's deconstruct the timeline, looking at how we got from Point A to Point B and from Point B to Point C and so on. This helps us see our main drivers—the places in our hearts and minds that have governed our choices in the past and may continue to do so in the future *unless we change*. These motivators have been hard for us to perceive in our daily lives, but the repetitions and patterns of our past choices are now made clear to us. They are important clues as to how we might create a different outcome.

Something else happens as we look at our lives from this distance. We can't help but wish we had done at least some things differently. Creating a life timeline frequently brings up the ill-considered choices of our youth that have come to define us. *How could we have made such a choice? What were we thinking?* But we have to remember that these choices made sense *at the time.* They reflect the individuals we were, just as choices made going forward will reflect the individuals we have become.

Our timeline gives us our marching orders, pointing the way to the future. If we don't like the choices we have made, we can change things, write new life stories. No, we don't get to go back and fix things. If our life story doesn't please us, we can write our stories from the page we're on, based upon our new knowledge and understanding. That's the point of our journey: to begin to see how our choices have helped us or prevented us from becoming our authentic selves.

Making Meaning

Hunting in the past for clues has helped us understand our main drivers. We now have an understanding of why certain choices were made, but only a surface understanding. We still haven't figured out what it all adds up to, *what it means.* From our spot on the yellow brick road, we have a need for greater understanding. We want to see our lives as more than a continuum or dots on a line.

To get beyond the surface impression of our lives, we have to bring our whole self to our interpretation of events, processing information we have received at deeper levels. It is not that each single event in our life is unimportant; it is that the key to understanding ourselves lies in seeing how these events intertwine and have themes and stories that have come to define us. We are not defined by just one thing we did or person we knew; we are, in the end, defined by all of these things—what we have put out into the world *en masse* and taken from it.

Our view of ourselves from the yellow brick road is not a simplistic or self-limiting one. It infers meaning that goes beyond how we have acted from day to day and gives us permission to create a whole-life interpretation of who and what we are. This is very freeing and forgiving. It is also true.

A Different Story

In the opening of Alice Sebold's remarkable book *The Lovely Bones*, we meet Susie Salmon, the 14-year-old narrator of the story. Susie has just been murdered and cannot leave the earth. From her unusual vantage point, she tries to make sense of her life and struggles to gain understanding and perspective on what has just happened. She looks on as her family is torn apart by grief. She sees her mother and father consumed by guilt and obsessed with solving her murder. She cannot go to her final resting place until she knows that they will be okay.

But then, slowly, Susie begins to see things differently. She comes to understand that to make sense of what has happened in the past, she must transform her understanding of it. It is only when she sees the connections that have developed since her death—the "lovely bones" that have grown around her absence—that she is able to perceive the totality of life, the chain that connects us all. That is what finally gives her peace and lets her leave the earth for her final resting place. She has found a way to transform the direst of circumstances into something deeply lovely and meaningful.

Remember when Professor Marvel showed Dorothy her home and family through a magic crystal? From our new perspective, we too have the magical ability to gain a deeper understanding of our lives as a whole. We see beyond our difficult circumstances or perceived mistakes. We create meaning out of what has happened, even the most tragic events, by putting them in context of what we now know to be true. Yes, we can even re-interpret past events according to what each has meant to us over the long term. We can see how each life experience helped us grow into the person we are now. We can honor this transformation and then move beyond it.

On the road to Oz we read the signs that take us from a two-dimensional understanding to a three-dimensional, deeply personal yet broader view of our lives. As Dorothy learned when her house landed in Oz, the details of how we got here are important, but they are only a starting place. Meaning is derived from what we make of the details and how we use them to continue our story as we begin to express ourselves in the world as authentic individuals.

Reading the Signs of the Road

Sorcery is defined as "the human control of supernatural agencies or the forces of nature." Who doesn't think a little magic will help them gain control of their lives? Who doesn't want a crystal ball to see into the future? We would all probably like to be able to will things to happen and many of us read books that tell us we can. Certainly, there is power in positive thinking. And the Law of Attraction has been shown to have merit. Yet on the road to Oz we learn that the best way to make magic in our lives is through our own skill and initiative.

We have set out on this road with no magic other than the magic of our own special powers. The Wizard can't help us unless we first help ourselves. We have to rely on our own cleverness and insight to negotiate the signs and symbols before us. Surprisingly, once on the road, anything we create out of our whole being gets us exactly where we want and need to be. Sure, one way or the other our lives will unfold. But why not use the magic we were born with—the special gifts that are ours alone? When we learn to rely on our own instincts, resources, and imagination, we begin to *get* why this road is worth traveling. We see what our magic can create.

Stories We Tell Ourselves

One of the best ways to move forward on the road to Oz is by listening to the language of our dreams. We have already seen the power of dreams to change lives. Now we see that our dreams contain vital clues to our past and our future. We might think of them as stories we tell ourselves, designed to help us break down barriers and create significant change. Yes, they often come to us in a language that is difficult to understand. They contain symbols that take some work to decode, but once we do, it is well worth it.

Some dreams are more powerful than others. These are the ones that disturb us, even wake us up at night. Or, they may repeat themselves for weeks or months, or even years. When we wake up from these dreams we may feel transformed in some way. It is very similar to how Dorothy feels when she first wakes up in Oz. *What just happened*? We try to replay the dream in our mind, but the closer we get to it, the more its details and meanings elude us.

Fortunately, on the road to Oz we get to play with the images in our dreams, much as a child plays with Lego bricks, building and rebuilding the symbols until they start to make sense. The language in dreams presents itself as a puzzle we are meant to solve, and when we do, the *aha* moment can transform us. Our dreams deliver brand new ideas and give us access to hidden parts of ourselves. We unlock doors that have been closed to us and walk right through, as if the barriers were never there. What at first seemed incomprehensible is suddenly clear. Why hadn't we seen it before?

Often the images in our dreams are symbols of ideas. For example, bridges may symbolize our need to get through a difficult life passage, and gates may symbolize (as mine did) the need to get unstuck in some part of our lives. The symbolic language of our dreams is meant only for us. The gate that appeared over and over again in my dream may have meant something different to someone else, but for me, it had a very specific meaning that I had to decipher. It forced me to confront an issue I might have avoided, enabling me to gain the courage to move forward with my life.

On the road to Oz, our dreams may become even more vivid and colorful, as we struggle to break through to our authentic self. They may stir up memories from the past stored for years in our subconscious, only to re-emerge now as a clue to what is happening in our present that needs to take us to the future. If we want to grow, we have to read these messages from our subconscious. In our dreams, there are wicked witches and other frightening things we cannot escape. But fortunately, in real life we can!

The Magic of Moving Forward

We are ready to move forward to a brighter future. But first we have to get comfortable again in the present moment, the very last point in our timeline. Looking toward Oz from some point in the past will only result in muddled or stale thinking. Again, taking the long view of our lives, the *past* has no *present* role in the *future* we are trying to create.

And yet, as alert and aware as we are on the yellow brick road, sometimes we may find ourselves slipping into old habits— moving backward instead of forward. Luckily, there are all kinds of signs on the road to Oz to alert us when this is happening or about to happen. Looking out for these signs is the best way I know to make magic in our lives. We can fling open the gates and break down the barriers that have been holding us back. We can move from a stuck position into a *let's go!* attitude. This is our own kind of magic.

Here's a list of the signs to watch out for that show us we may be moving backward instead of forward. Don't panic if any of these occur; just know that on the yellow brick road we are not only capable of spotting reverse trends in our behavior, we are equally capable of making the changes that will get us moving forward again.

Sign #1: We Sound Like a Broken Record

Do we hear ourselves continually talking about our past hurts? If so, this is probably keeping us from moving forward. The talk lets us continue to ask ourselves why. *Why did he leave me? Why didn't I get this job? Why didn't my parent understand me better?* No matter how well we understand what happened in the past, we keep searching for the one answer that will make moving forward easier. We struggle with what I call "uncertainty of meanings," and believe that replaying the same old record will ultimately yield a solution that frees us from the past.

The truth is, there is rarely a single answer to our *why* questions that will forever put them to rest. Yet we keep on replaying the dramas of our past, if only because it feels safer to us than abandoning the broken record and traveling down an uncertain road. That is why I always allow my patients to talk about the past and do not hurry them along. I have come to understand that replaying meanings is all part of the process of moving forward. Quieting our minds does require that we first shake them up a bit until we are satisfied that no amount of questioning will yield a surefire solution. The shakeup is necessary, as long as it ultimately gets us moving again.

As Einstein once said, "Insanity is doing the same things but expecting different results." If we expect change in our lives, we have to shake up the *known* and then move to the *unknown*. It's the only way forward.

Sign #2: We're Thinking Inside the Box

Thinking inside the box is a sure sign that we are stuck in the past. That's because no matter what we know to be true, we keep coming up with the same old solutions to solve our problems. What about trying a new approach? If we want change in our lives, we have to let our desires and growing needs out of the box. We can't keep bumping our heads against the same old wall. We have to find new solutions.

Sometimes we are stuck in boxes designed by our social selves. Moving out of these boxes requires that we get beyond social expectation and pressure. For example, before I decided to return to school to pursue a psychology degree, I worked in sales. One day I told my sales manager that I planned to leave the job and return to school to become a psychologist. I will never forget his response: "A psychologist! What do you want to do *that* for?" Fortunately, I did not let his negativity discourage me. I let myself out of the box of the social self and began the long journey of trusting myself.

Sign #3: We're Standing at the Starting Gate

This is where many of us get stuck—right at the starting gate. Even if we have yearnings and dreams that we would like to explore, we remain stranded at the starting gate, unable to take a bold leap into the future. One major reason for this is a lack of faith—faith that things will work out and go right for us, or faith in our own decisions.

Part of the problem is that we put too much pressure on ourselves to achieve instant success. We imagine the worst outcome, playing out our losses before they even happen! We have to take a leap of faith—to trust the process and let our faith in ourselves, and/or in a higher power, move us forward. Faith gives us the strength to take a risk and move forward, no matter how frightened or insecure we may feel.

Sign #4: We're Feeling Out of Sync

Life isn't easy, but it shouldn't be all that hard either. When we are stuck in the past, things do seem harder. There's little movement or flow to our activities. Nothing feels straightforward, and every door we try to pull open seems to push back on us. These are signs that we have changes to make and the universe, or whatever we wish to call it, isn't going to cooperate unless we do. We need to get back in sync.

Before I started the blog *Psychology in Everyday Life,* I tried many things that for one reason or another just didn't work out. I was stuck until I started to do what came most naturally to me— that is to communicate ideas that help people thrive. I was suddenly in sync with myself and everything and everyone. I was in the right place and moving forward again. I was on my way to Oz.

Sign #5: We Bear the Mark of Dracula

There is perhaps no more telltale sign of being stuck in outworn ideas and actions than feeling like all the life is being drained out of us. We have all experienced times when a friend, lover, job, or activity started to take more from us in energy, motivation, and support than it gave back. It's generally tough to leave these situations, as we tend to remain loyal to the paths we have carved out for ourselves. Even if we know something isn't right, we're reluctant to change the course midstream.

So we push on, drained of life. We feel trapped and hopeless and have little motivation to continue—and yet we persist. We continue to travel down a road that isn't right for us rather than admit defeat or try something new. We're moving along, and yet we're just as stuck as our friend who is stalled at the starting gate. To get unstuck we have to honor the physical and mental signs that are telling us that something needs to change.

Sign #6: We Don't Know Whether to Leave or Stay

The worst kind of stuck is to be trapped—or rather to trap ourselves—in toxic relationships. We know that a person isn't good for us, yet we can't let them go. Unable to decide whether to stay or move on, we remain in limbo. Clearly, this kind of waffling doesn't get us any closer to Oz.

What are the signs that a relationship has passed its sell-by date? One is our own behavior. Are we acting authentically in this relationship? Can we be true to ourselves and still be with this person? If the answer to this question is no, it's a sign to us that we aren't meant to bring this person into our future. We may even know this but be holding on because we fear letting go of this relationship. If so, taking a risk is the only way to move forward.

Sign #7: We Frequent Our Old Haunts

Are we still visiting the old places we used to go, and do we have trouble letting go of them? Are we still actively engaged in a sport or activity we used to share with a past friend or lover? We don't have to stop this activity, as long as it is something we still enjoy. But we have to bring something new to it, something that relates to our life in the present.

For example, let's say we enjoy attending classical concerts together, and this is an activity we would like to continue to enjoy on our own. Our challenge is to try and find something new in the experience, something about it that is uniquely ours. We don't bury the memory, but we coat it with a fresh layer of paint. In this way, we honor the past as we walk into the future.

A Step Closer to Oz

We have seen that there is a practical side to this journey to Oz and so much we can do, positively and proactively, to increase our chances for success. The road is a magical place, but only due to our own efforts. We have inside us what no amount of sorcery or wizardry or even help from others can give us—a wellspring of ideas, impulses, and creativity that is uniquely our own. We have an ability no one else has and a unique perspective we can apply to our own experience of life.

Many of the patients who arrive in my office or readers of my blog *Psychology in Everyday Life* are searching for answers. They want the best for their lives and wonder how they will achieve it. I know that just by wanting their lives to change, they have taken the first step toward making that happen. Wanting to grow and change means we have already been paying attention to clues and signs, and learning the magic and artistry of believing in ourselves. For those of us who have begun to do this, Oz is now closer than ever.

Chapter Seven:

Lessons from the Poppy Field

We have learned how to navigate and make the most of our journey. Now we have to begin the process of preparing for success. This means not only understanding what success really looks like, but developing a philosophy that protects us from the traps, tricks, and self-defeating ideas that could stop us in our tracks. Yes, we are eager to make our way in the world; but once we get that first taste of the fruits of our efforts, it is possible to get sidetracked or even duped into believing we are already in Oz, when in fact, we have far to go.

Perhaps we have begun to act in the world as authentic beings. We may even have started to create an authentic life that represents who we are as individuals. Just as we begin to take these first positive steps, something happens that affects our commitment to the journey: We get our first glimpse of the Emerald City, glittering in the distance, and suddenly we can't wait, we want to be there—*right now!* The lure of a "good-enough life" is hard to resist—much harder than anything we may have faced before. It will take all of our strength and determination to continue on the path we have set out for ourselves. Now, we must work harder than ever to stay fully awake on the journey.

Dorothy was as close to Oz as we are now when she nearly lost her way—so close she could see the tall towers of the Emerald City looming in the distance. Drawn to its beauty and promise, she ran as fast as she could through a field of bright red poppies that blocked her way. Suddenly, she began to lose energy, and soon she was so tired all she wanted to do was sleep. Of course, she had no idea that a trap had been set for her by the Wicked Witch of the West to prevent her from getting to Oz. It was only the quick thinking of the Scarecrow, the Tin Woodman, and the Lion that saved her from the spell of the poppy field.

It may seem strange, but the closer we get to Oz, the more we are in danger of watching our dreams be erased. Just when we start to understand what we want and need, we may suddenly lack the drive to keep moving toward it. It can be hard to find that last bit of hope necessary to create a life of meaning and purpose, even when people we love are rooting for us and the bright lights of Oz glow in the distance.

Resisting the Spell of Defeat

By now we must realize that the fragrance and beauty of the poppy field are deadly traps to reel us in. Were the poppy field less tempting, we might not be inclined to settle for what we have and remain right where we are; in other words, stop growing. These temptations that call out to us are powerful forces—not the twists, turns, and tornadoes we are accustomed to handling. These forces are subtle, confusing, even mesmerizing, and may divert our attention just when we need it most. As potent as a witch's spell, they threaten to sabotage all of our hard work—if we let them.

The good news is, the spell that puts us in the poppy field is reversible. It may require a new understanding of our drives and goals, and yes, we will have a bit of work to do. But even if we have fallen asleep, we can wake ourselves up, dust ourselves off, and turn our lives around. All we have to do to get ourselves moving again is understand the traps that first seduced and derailed us.

Trap #1: Mistaken Goals

Many of us start down the road to Oz without a complete understanding of the journey. We are anxious to "find ourselves" and speak likewise. But we have grown up in a society that defines success in material terms, and that has rubbed off on us. In theory, we may understand the idea of carving out an authentic life that expresses who we are. But somewhere in our heart and mind we are still attached to finding the end goal—that signal that tells us we have reached success. We want the visible signs of a job well done.

If this is the goal we are reaching for, the journey to Oz can't

96

help but lead to disappointment. For although getting to Oz is about finding the path to an authentic life, the journey doesn't ever stop there. Getting to Oz does not refer to arriving at some end goal, but to the fact that we are *always* getting to Oz. It is not a one-time journey, but an ongoing process, a continuous evaluation of emerging energies inside of us that are constantly seeking self-expression.

Some of us fall into the trap of the poppy field because we are fooled into thinking that arriving in Oz will be a reward for our efforts. With any outward signs of success, we begin treating ourselves as winners and act as if there is now nothing else left for us to do. We forget that getting to Oz is an ongoing process and that the journey to Oz never really ends until we die. If we are human beings and we are alive, there will always be more to do, for that is the nature of human existence. New desires will continue to emerge in us, until we take our last breath.

Robert Frost said it this way:

> The woods are lovely, dark and deep.
> But I have promises to keep,
> And miles to go before I sleep,
> And miles to go before I sleep.

The traps that we fall into now lure us with a compelling alternative to more hard work and psychological processing. Yet, if we move on, the rewards are far greater. We leave the woods that are "lovely, dark, and deep," by resisting their spell, with our hearts and minds intact and fully engaged. We know we have "miles to go before [we] sleep." We continue to be awake and present in our lives, focused on maintaining the goals we have set for ourselves.

Trap #2: Questioning the Value of our Efforts

Our very first glimpse of Oz may be fleeting—just enough to make us realize how hard it has been to get to this point, but a none-too-pleasing reminder of how far we have yet to go. We have certainly worked hard, paid bills, and tried to be responsible, decent human beings. But how far has this taken us? For those of us whose lives are not what we had hoped for, not very far at all. We may begin to question the value of our efforts. Will they ever produce the results we are aiming for?

The film *Biutiful,* starring Javier Bardem, tells the story of Uxbal, a single father of two. His life has been a never-ending battle, from his abusive relationship with the mother of his children, to his fight to lead a straight life amidst the chaos and crime that is all around him. One day he receives a diagnosis of terminal cancer and is given only a few months to live. He decides he must try for something in this world—so he hires a good woman to care for his children and leaves money to poor factory workers. In the end, both of these noble efforts backfire and Uxbal dies, convinced that this is a world in which the criminals thrive while the innocent, the poor, and the weak are destined to suffer.

Uxbal's last act may seem desperate and tragic, but looked at another way, we may see it as glorious and yes, *biutiful!* The film asks an important existential question: What is the value of our efforts? Are we rewarded for our hard work, and if not, why not just give it all up, wander into a field of poppies, and fall asleep? After all, when we look around or read the news we may observe, as Uxbal did, that self-oriented, psychologically and spiritually undeveloped individuals seem to thrive by cheating, lying, and harming other people, while good, hard-working people are just trying to do the best they can to survive.

Should we just give up at this point or should we continue to strive to lead an authentic life? The answer to this question lies in how we define success. For those of us on the journey to Oz, success is not in the *getting,* but in the *striving.* If we use this definition of success, then by any measure Uxbal led an exemplary life. Even with the knowledge that his work on this earth was nearly done, he went as far as he possibly could to ensure his children's safety in the world. Perhaps his last desperate act saved them from repeating his failures; we will never know.

No matter our plight, as human beings we are designed to unfold our best individual selves at our worst times. If we stop doing this, it is only because we are in the poppy field and no longer awake. Of course, we can allow ourselves to succumb and give up—to fall asleep. We can stop our psychological process from unfolding or we can continue to open ourselves to experience to see if there is more unfolding to do. If we do the latter, as Uxbal did, we are living our best life, but as part of a process, not a destination. It is what we do, not where we get, that counts. Too bad Uxbal couldn't understand this.

Choosing to stay on the road to Oz means we refuse to buy into other people's definition of life's true value. Yes, there are people who appear to have it all and not to have worked very hard for it. They have more money, status, and power than we will ever have. But we have to continue to keep in mind what it is that we value most and what we are moving toward. The road to Oz is paved with gold, but it is a different sort of gold than we may have thought. It is the gold of psychological and spiritual development—of self-worth, not monetary worth. In other words, it is gold worth having.

Trap #3: Buying into the Good-Enough Life

For many of us, getting that first taste of what feels like success is more powerful than any drug could ever be. Our successes, especially the material kind, cause us to turn a blind eye to the needs and desires that are rising up inside us. We are lulled into apathy with regard to our psychological process. In our hearts and minds, we know that there may be more to do, but we quit trying, especially because what is left to do is usually the hardest part. Why keep trying when we think we may already be there?

Perhaps we feel we have done a good job up until this point, making authentic choices about our friendships and career paths. With our first glimpse of Oz, we may begin to think that we deserve more than we already have and that we have earned the right to begin to enjoy the fruits of our labors. The good-enough life comes and claims us as soon as we begin to feel that sense of entitlement. We are lured into believing it is okay to stop honoring the psychological needs and yearnings that are still inside us, still wanting and waiting to be expressed.

How do we know we are leading the good-enough life? Simple—sooner or later, it lets us down. How could it not? It lures us precisely because it asks so little of us and gets so little from us in return. It is as if we are simply biding our time, awaiting our marching orders to get moving again. Like chess pieces on a board, we wait for the next order from above, with no idea what it may be. In this way, the good-enough life neither challenges us nor permits us to grow. We may be financially secure, but we cannot be emotionally or psychologically stable in a life that offers so little to our growth and development.

Even if we don't pull ourselves out of the good-enough life, one way or another it will come to an end. Sometimes, it is with a jolt: A sudden illness or lack of energy brings us down, *hard.* One day we have trouble getting ourselves out of bed in the morning. Soon we find that we are spending our days sleepwalking through life with our eyes closed—literally, not fully awake. Our needs and desires are churning. Not having been given their true expression, they now prevent us from fully engaging with the life we are in. As they strain for release, they come out in unsettling and even destructive ways.

Fortunately, many of us respond to these physical issues and will now choose to search out the help we need. Whoever it is that comes to our rescue—a doctor, counselor, friend, or lover—merely has to re-introduce us to ourselves. This is all the impetus we need to wake up and pay attention to our true yearnings so that we can get back on the road to Oz.

Trap #4: Failing to Recognize Fear

Falling asleep during this part of our journey may be a sign that we are afraid of something. Perhaps we sense an unmet need that we must bring out into the open but for one reason or another cannot. "Sleeping" is a way to avoid what we fear. This is not the lions-and-tigers-and-bears type of fear that lurks in the imagination. This is fear that is difficult to identify and makes us uncomfortable in some way. The more unconsciously we face our lives the more it is likely to surface.

It is likely that Dorothy had many fears when she caught that first glimpse of Oz: *Is there really a Wizard of Oz? Will he agree to see me when I get there? What if he can't help me? What if I never find my way back to Kansas?* No doubt, her list of fears went on and on, and we can understand why. She was trapped in a world she did not understand and in which she felt she had little power. With success literally around the corner, she felt understandably frightened about her ability to achieve it.

If only our own fears were so easy to isolate. But the fear we are likely to have at this point in our journey may be difficult to pin down. We have trouble understanding fear that is associated with success or fulfillment, as it seems so unlikely to fear something that is so overwhelmingly positive. We may also fear things from long ago and far away, and these fears may surface now, as we often leave the thing we fear most for the end.

Victoria's Story

Victoria came to see me in what she described as a depressed state. She was having trouble getting out of bed in the morning— something that was unusual for her, as she was a naturally vivacious person, engaged with life. She explained to me that her melancholic state had come on suddenly, just after she had accomplished an important goal. I saw its roots in a much earlier part of her story—her first plan to come to America.

Now thirty-five, she had arrived in America years earlier with only a high school education and a strong desire to make her own way in the world. Despite the difficulties of learning a new language and customs, she had found a terrific job and worked hard to reach each rung on the ladder. She had done well, proven herself along the way, and there could be no doubt in anyone's mind, least of all her own, that she had reached the goals she had set for herself. Why then was she suddenly unable to move on?

Together, Victoria and I worked it through. I explained to her that even though she had attained her worldly goals, there were likely still inner yearnings and desires that needed free expression.

Achieving her material goals had made her stop looking inside. As a result, she was now sleepwalking through her life. Her unmet needs and desires important to her emotional health were being ignored. Victoria needed to reach back inside to see what else was there.

Victoria and I examined the whole of her life, not just the material trappings of success. Slowly, she began to see that in putting all of her energy into her career, she had covered over a fear that just grew deeper over time—the fear of romantic love and intimacy. It had started when she was very young and experienced the breakup of her parents' marriage. Now that Victoria was closest to fulfilling her worldly goals, these early childhood fears were beginning to rise to the surface.

Victoria's deep yearnings forced her to slow down and pay attention to what was going on inside of her. Once she faced her fears, she was able to continue her journey in a healthier way, paying full attention to all aspects of her being and bringing her whole self to Oz.

Trap #5: Thinking Only of Ourselves

In Lakota native Indian culture, the greatest honor was to become a Shirt Wearer. When men like Crazy Horse and Sitting Bull donned the shirt, they were declaring their commitment to the greater good—a vow to lead by example. Shirt Wearers were ordinary people just like us, but they had emotionally and spiritually developed to a point where they could exercise wisdom and control over their behavior. They were expected to rise above personal matters, and if they did not, they were stripped of their Shirt Wearer role.

We get trapped in the poppy field when we think only of ourselves and fail to perceive the greater good. To get out of the poppy field, all we have to do is become a Shirt Wearer by embracing those ideals. When we no longer live just for ourselves, we are less likely to be trapped by the temptations of security, or the good-enough life. We accept that even if we have reached a degree of self-fulfillment and caught our first glimpse of Oz, our work is not done. We still have to use our gifts to inspire, mentor, and promote other individuals.

The more that we embrace these values, the further we are led from the path of the ego (and the perils of the poppy field). At this point in our journey, we can begin to use our gifts and talents in the world, as opposed to holding onto them so tightly. Sharing what we have learned thus far helps us to promote the culture of the yellow brick road, which in turn helps us to complete our journey. We stay out of the poppy field by paying it forward!

Developing a New Mindset

We have referred to our descent into the poppy field as a kind of sleep, but in reality it is more like a death—a death of the spirit. Earlier, we spoke of developing a warhorse spirit to guide us. That was what was needed then, as we were still in the process of developing a plan and still plotting our route along the yellow brick road. Now, something else is required, not something that gets us on the road but something that *keeps us there.*

My mother often said to me, "Deborah, we must do what we must do." The implication of this simple idea didn't really occur to me until much later in life, when my faith in my own path began to falter. I started to wonder if it was all worth it—all the effort and hard work. Was what I was doing really going to lead me to an authentic and fully realized life? My mother's words came back to me (as they often do). They told me that the only option open to me was to plow ahead and *do what I must do.*

From Creator to Cultivator

To do what we must do, we now have to go from being a creator to being a cultivator. Now we will do whatever is necessary for us to thrive, no more and no less. This keeps us strong and focused. We do this, knowing that whatever grows from here will take us further. We may sense that Oz is up ahead, but we do not turn our attention to the finish line. Instead, we focus on what is in front of us, cultivating its full potential.

Now it is not a *warhorse* spirit but a *plow-horse* spirit that is required to help us tend the field we have created. A plow-horse spirit allows us to keep our heads down as we continue each day to do what we must do. We may get our first glimpse of Oz, yet we recognize that it all starts right here—that whatever we make happen from this moment forward will take us exactly where we need to be. We dare not leave our field unattended. We know we must continue to do whatever is required to make sure that it thrives.

From Cultivator to Storyteller

As cultivators, each of us has our own field to tend. And yet—at this point there is much we can learn from the experience of others. In my own life I have discovered how essential it is to read and listen and get inspired. Stories stimulate my imagination and become valuable in my work as a psychologist, as I find they speak best for the human spirit and condition. I have tried to share as many stories as possible throughout this book, using them to help us diagnose our own personal challenges.

Perhaps the best inspiration of all comes from the stories that are handed down through our families—from generation to generation. No story has had a more profound impact on my life than the story of my parents, Mitchell and Mabel Khoshaba. Their story has been a source of great inspiration to me, giving me hope when I could not find it and providing the impetus I needed to keep on moving toward an authentic life.

It has helped me pull myself out of the poppy field countless times and given me the strength to endure.

Mitchell and Mabel's Story

I remember the truck pulling up to our two-story flat in Chicago to take my mother, father, sisters, and brothers to Elk Grove Village, a suburb of Chicago, Illinois. I was only seven. The move was a big event in my young life, but I had no idea at the time what it meant for my parents, nor did I understand all that had happened to make such a move possible. For instance, I had no idea what my parents had sacrificed to get to this point, nor did I understand how far, psychologically and emotionally, they had journeyed from their Iranian homeland.

Each of my parents had endured hardships greater than any I would ever know. My father's challenges had come early at the hands of a tyrannical father who abused him throughout his childhood. It took all his strength to outgrow this abuse. My mother had been forced into an arranged marriage with my father at the age of fifteen, thus putting an abrupt end to her youth. This change in her life did not discourage her or leave her bitter; it only made her surer and stronger, and more determined to follow her own path as soon as she was able.

My mother was fortunate in one thing, though: my father turned out to be a hard worker. He hauled cargo in Iran, trying to save up enough money so that they could go to America and pursue the American Dream. Finally, in 1949, at the age of twenty-five, Mitchell traded in his Mack diesel truck for eighty Persian carpets, and my parents set off for America. They were young, hopeful, and excited to trade their challenging life in Iran for a piece of the American pie.

Like many immigrants, my parents soon learned that life in America was anything but idyllic and had its own share of frustrations and disappointments. Still, they never abandoned their dreams. No matter what hardships they faced, they looked for the good in themselves and others, and found a way to endure. They lived this way because it was the only way they knew how to live. It was their way, the source of wisdom and wonder that protected their lives and, eventually, the lives of their children.

Did Mitchell and Mabel eventually reach Oz? Yes, I am sure they would say that they did. I prefer to think of it this way: It was not any outward measure of success, but their ability to respond positively to life circumstances that was their greatest achievement. That is a goal worth striving for.

Going the Distance

There is a medical condition that can occur in the first years of life called "failure to thrive." Most children gain weight and grow quickly, but not in all cases. Some fail to meet the expected standards of growth. This can happen for many reasons, but always includes a failure to grow as expected. For doctors, it is a tricky road to get children back to healthy growing patterns. Thankfully, in many cases, it does happen.

The longer we stay in our poppy field, the harder it will be to restore a healthy way of life and get back to our journey. What we have is a kind of failure to thrive. Although we still breathe and exist on the planet, we have reached a point of diminishing returns and no longer derive benefit from the life we have created. There is much that remains available to us, but for one reason or another, we no longer reach for it. We are alive but no longer living.

Life goes on because it always does. It goes on whether we grab it by both hands and make the most of it, or decide to lag behind and wait for change to come. It continues, in one way or another, for this is the way of human existence. The only choice we have at this point is whether to simply let life happen to us or to change and grow by our own design. The knowledge we have gained thus far on the yellow brick road has granted us this choice; but it isn't enough to just know something; we still have to *act.*

Quitting Is Not an Option

One thing about Dorothy—she wasn't a quitter. No wicked old witch could intimidate her; no flying monkey could cause her to cancel her plans. But that's the point: Dorothy had something to fight against! Could it be that it was facing her demons, real and imaginary, that spurred her on? What if there are no flying monkeys in our path? No lions and tigers and bears, real or imaginary, to dissuade us from pursuing our dreams? If we don't have to fight our way upward from log-cabin roots, if our path is a little too easy, can we still keep our footing? Can we create our own internal pressure to keep us moving on to Oz? And for those of us who do have to fight our way up from difficult beginnings, can we give ourselves a way to move onward when we lose our way?

We can if we want to.

We were able to get this far on our journey. To keep ourselves going requires something more. It requires *will*. If I were to impart only one message in this book it would be this: We cannot get anywhere in life without having the will to move forward—without a decision to thrive! I have provided encouraging ideas about how we can get ourselves going once we have gotten off track. But none of this can happen *unless we want it to*. We have to *want* to get to Oz at this point and we have to *want* to move our lives along. As simple as this sounds, that is the great secret of this part of the journey, and the one that will help us find our way back onto the yellow brick road. We must summon up our will, and then we will move on.

The spirit of my parents must also reside in me, for I do not know how to quit. Throughout my life, I have moved through challenge after challenge simply because I have given myself no other option. Whenever I find myself questioning the value of pursuing an authentic life, I find something to move me forward. Frequently, it is the spirit, joy, and triumph of my parents that comes back to me. I picture them setting foot on American soil with everything ahead of them—their own version of Oz just around the corner. I think of them making their way through hardships, determined to endure.

What part of success in life is attributable simply to a refusal to give up? We may never know. The world is full of such stories—from the annals of science, art, invention, and politics—of those who simply would not take no for an answer. What we do know for certain is practice does tend to make us better, if not perfect, and by doing something over and over again, we not only reveal our strength, but our spirit and will to continue, despite the odds that mount against us.

Renewing Our Pledge

Perhaps it would be a good idea at this point to remind ourselves of the pledge we made when we first set foot on the yellow brick road. At that time we committed to unfolding the truest expression of our desires and goals at every stage of our life, no matter how far we had come or how much further we had to go. We promised to stay awake to the process inside of us as observing, feeling authors of our experience.

We continue our journey on the yellow brick road with the certainty in our hearts and minds that there is no place we would rather be. By renewing our commitment to the course we have set for ourselves, we pledge that no matter how far along we are, we can yet be inspired to go further, to do more, for that is what our journey is all about—not the reward for our efforts, but the joy that comes from moving forward. From the poppy field back to the yellow brick road, we keep these valuable thoughts in mind.

Chapter Eight:

The Secret of the Ruby Slippers

Throughout this book I have referred to getting to Oz as going home to what is authentic and true—not what is safe and familiar. Going home, at least in the context of this book, has meant getting to what is true for us, which means discarding any former beliefs that may have held us back. With the ruby slippers on her feet, Dorothy always had the ability to go home—and so did we! But first we had to take a great journey of self-discovery and transformation. We had to make a decision to love ourselves unconditionally and take those first tentative steps toward Oz.

We began our journey in the enchanted forest, where at first we were afraid and sought safety and protection. But soon we realized that our souls strived for something more—something far different from what we could ever get in the outer world or by reaching back to the security of our childhood. We made our way out, and before long we were traveling down the road, using the signs and symbols all around us to release our creativity and remove the barriers that prevented us from stepping into our true self. We resisted the seductive powers of the poppy field and remained true to our purpose.

Our perseverance has earned us the right to use the great power of the ruby slippers. What will we find when we tap our heels together and arrive in our version of home? Will it be all that we hoped for, or will we, like Dorothy, have to separate fact from fantasy, truth from illusion? The secret of the ruby slippers is that they bring us to a new kind of home—one where we have power we did not know we possessed, and one where we meet our authentic self, stripped of illusion. Let's take a look at what it feels like to land in Oz, and how we can make the most of all that awaits us now that we're home.

There's No Place Like Home

When Dorothy's house landed on top of the Wicked Witch of the East, she was immediately looked up to as a powerful being—more powerful than the evil force she had destroyed. It must have seemed strange to her that everyone saw her as mighty and powerful, when she still saw herself as small and meek. But the ruby slippers that magically appeared on her feet at this time symbolized the seeds of real power that had begun to take shape within her and would continue to materialize on her journey.

To understand her special powers and earn the right to use them, Dorothy would have to complete a personal odyssey of self-discovery and transformation. We know that she has been transformed because she tells Glinda there is no point in seeking our heart's desire beyond our own backyard, "because if it isn't there, then we never really lost it in the first place." Dorothy finally *gets* that home is a place where we are finally at home with ourselves.

Like Dorothy, we have had to earn the right to use our own ruby slippers. We delivered ourselves from the perils—the lions and tigers and bears—and emerged with the realization and confidence to be at home with our selves. This is not the home we left behind. In our new stage of psychological development, we are now at home on a higher level. It is not so much that we are wiser than before, but that we are truer to our needs, making choices that we can only make from our new vantage point in Oz.

At Home with Ourselves

What does it mean to be at home with our selves? It means that we have a sense of comfort with who we are as individuals. Now, we are naturally, authentically, and truly our own, without compromise. We accept ourselves unconditionally, with all of our flaws and limitations. All of our illusions have now been stripped away. We have learned that where there is self-love there is no longer a need for pretense—only a clear and focused path to a happier, healthier life.

My own journey home began with a recurring dream. I was alone in the fog, searching for what I then called "home." I wanted my home to be a safe and sheltering place that would protect me and cradle me with support, as my home never did. Like most of us do at this early age, I was looking outside myself for the answers. I'd tell myself, *I have to become financially successful to clear the fog that has blinded me and made me so afraid.* But as I matured, learned, and opened up my self-knowledge, I understood better what I had been desperately seeking in the fog. It was not "home" in the way we usually think of it, but rather the comfort and security that comes with living an authentic life. Gradually, I came to understand that no amount of material security would ever provide me with that sense of comfort. I would be lost and searching—and I use the word "lost" in the most personal sense of that word—until I connected with my authentic self.

When we are at home with ourselves, it means we have learned the importance of valuing ourselves as whole and fully functioning individuals with a unified way of being in the world. No longer dependent upon others, we are able to make the best use of all that we have—what we were born with and the values, beliefs, and talents we have acquired on our journey. Now we are transparent, our inner lives and our inner light right out in front for the world to see.

Being at home also gives us the right to use our personal power. We can now choose for ourselves and trust that our choices will lead us in the right direction. These choices are as critical to our new stage of psychological development as the ones that got us here. They allow us to show the world the truest expression of who we are.

Opening the Door to Self-Knowledge

We began our journey to Oz with the belief that it was possible to transform our lives, but we did not know how we would accomplish it. Like Dorothy, we could only imagine ourselves as whole, happy individuals, in a beautiful place of deep self-knowledge and comfort. Fortunately, we had the ability to look beyond our everyday world for the signs and symbols that would take us all the way to our authentic self. Our beliefs were strong enough for us to stand up to many challenges. Even in unknown territory, we were able to remain ourselves throughout. Like Dorothy, we refused to compromise the belief that we could, if we persevered, find our way home.

In the classic story *The Odyssey,* the Greek hero Odysseus journeys home after the epic battle that is the fall of Troy. His perseverance, courage, and strength enable him to endure and triumph over many obstacles. Odysseus is the better for his travels, a wiser, more perceptive leader of his people than he might have been had he headed home right after the battle.

The word "odyssey" has come to mean a journey involving profound change—a true journey of the mind and heart. At the end of such a journey, we come home to ourselves, in all of our strengths and our weaknesses. Like Odysseus, we have gained self-knowledge, and that has given us a special kind of power. We are now able to be emotionally honest with ourselves and take responsibility for all the things we are and are not. In short, we have arrived home to a better version of ourselves.

This does not mean we are perfect. We all have parts of ourselves we don't especially like—things about ourselves we would like to change. Weren't the "thoughtless" Scarecrow, the "heartless" Tin Woodman, and the "cowardly" Lion all representations of the various parts of Dorothy that needed to evolve and did? The difference is, now we can face up to these behaviors—our fears, our frailties, and our conflicts—using the self-understanding we have gained along the way. Likewise, we get to see the good and untapped parts of ourselves—the creative urges that speak to our true purpose and, if expressed, can lead to deeper life meaning and fulfillment.

Sadly, some people never make the journey to Oz. They wear the ruby slippers for an entire lifetime, never learning how to use them. Instead, they buy into the trap of sacrificing psychological and spiritual *needs* for social and material *wants.* Always looking outside for the answers and never taking the time to look inside to see what is already there, they never really know or learn to trust themselves.

Blake's Story

Blake came to see me after a failed relationship, one of many in his life. At forty-three, Blake had never been able to maintain a successful partnership and felt that he would always be alone in the world. Despite his claim that he wished to marry if the right woman came along, that never seemed to happen.

For Blake, the right woman needed to be good-looking, career-oriented, and also interested in settling down. Throughout the years, he had chosen some remarkably capable women as girlfriends. Each of them was beautiful, had a successful career, and wanted to marry and have children with the right person. But in each case, as soon as the relationship started to move toward commitment, Blake would start to see these women's "flaws." They were either too much of one thing or not enough of the other. Blake was always the one to walk away.

Blake was commitment phobic in the classic sense. He was a short sprinter. In horse-racing terms: great out of the gate but falling short of the finish line. Women loved him because he was a dream mate—hanging on to their every word, interested in their feelings, and solely existing to make their lives better. But as soon as the relationship was moving toward commitment, he lost interest.

The first time I approached Blake with the idea that he might be resisting commitment, he became defensive. "No," he said. "I really do want to marry." And indeed he did. Yet he kept breaking off relationships with women who would have made good marital partners. It wasn't the flaws of his mates that did him in; Blake actually made some wise choices. It was his lack of self-knowledge that created his inability to form relationships. Blake could not see himself clearly, could not see the ways in which he was cutting off intimacy just as it began.

I worked with Blake for quite a while to try to help him see how he was sabotaging his own chances for happiness. I hoped he would be able to face himself squarely, but feared he would continue to make choices based upon a false version himself, leading to more heartbreak, despair, and disillusionment. There were things in Blake's past that might have caused his fear of intimacy, but his resistance to looking inside ultimately caused him to leave therapy, so I have no idea how things turned out for him.

Blake's psychological development was short-circuited because he could not connect to his own command central. He simply had no way to tune into his authentic yearnings and therefore could not act in a way that benefited his needs. As a result, he remained trapped in a disparate state in which his parts never fully integrated. Try as he would to see himself clearly, he could not see the *whole* Blake. He could not come home.

Why do so many of us find it difficult to open up the door to self-knowledge? Perhaps we are afraid of what we will see inside. It may be that no one ever told us how extraordinary we really are—or perhaps we were told this too frequently. Whatever the reason, it is true that many of us find it difficult to face ourselves squarely. From time to time, as in Blake's case, we may bump into our authentic selves, but only as a result of tragic downward turns of fate that suddenly force us to pay attention to our emotional and spiritual needs.

The great value in our journey to Oz is that we finally get to face the truth about ourselves—one that accurately reflects every facet of our being. As a result, we are glad to accept full responsibility for the decisions we make, because we know that they are an accurate reflection of who we truly are.

Becoming Wizards in Our Own Lives

What makes us wizards in our own lives? It is the knowledge that we have reached a level of psychological awareness that allows us to take responsibility for our own wellbeing. Knowledge is power, but it is also the stripping away of illusion. No longer can we hold on to the false illusion that anyone or anything will come in and fix us. Once we earn a certain level of psychological development, it is very hard to turn our back on ourselves. As wizards in our own lives, we now have the sole responsibility for our continued self-growth and development.

Part of this new level of self-knowledge is the understanding that we are who we believe we are. Yes, it is true. We can transform ourselves, but not by snapping our fingers or tapping our heels. We can change ourselves through the psychological process that allows us to genuinely alter our beliefs as we keep learning and growing. Each time we adapt our beliefs to our growing self-knowledge we enter into a new sphere of being. We say "yes" to each new stage of development, and slowly, not through magic but through paying attention to the process, we change our possibilities.

It is our beliefs that allow us to be wizards in our lives. They put us in places only we can imagine. If we dare to believe it, then we can build it, grow it, and make it happen. With our beliefs, we become as great and powerful as we will ourselves to be, capable of bringing our lives into balance and focus. More than anything else, getting to Oz puts us in touch with our beliefs and gives us the wisdom and maturity to transform them.

The Alchemist and the Wizard

What is the difference between an alchemist and a wizard? The wizard immediately makes things happen. With a snap of his fingers or a wave of his wand, he produces the desired result. The alchemist operates differently. He puts things together, tinkering and creating and mixing different substances, a little of this and a little of that, until he gets it just right. Alchemy is not instant magic but requires thinking, imagining, and the courage to see things through. It produces the desired transformation, but only through time and effort.

Growing into our new selves by getting to Oz has been an alchemical process: Gradual, deliberate, and completely within our control. It continues in this same vein throughout our lives. All we need to do is stay on top of what is happening as we move along on our travels and continue to notice the changes that are taking place.

For example, as we continue to move further along in our

psychological development, we may find that we are beginning to gravitate toward different types of relationships or that we are interested in new activities that are more aligned with who we are in the process of becoming. This process is important! We need to let it happen and not hold on too tight to outmoded beliefs that no longer fit who we are.

From Small and Meek to Great and Powerful

Dorothy began her journey to Oz with strong beliefs. She believed in a magical place over the rainbow where she could become her authentic self. What she did not believe—at least not yet—was that she had her own power to bring these things about and transform her life. On her journey to Oz Dorothy opened up her imagination, and consequently her world, ultimately leading to her complete psychological transformation.

The three friends Dorothy met on the road to Oz represented each critical new stage in her development:

> *The Scarecrow* represented Dorothy's belief that she was intelligent enough to make things happen.

> *The Tin Woodman* represented Dorothy's belief that she could get in touch with her true feelings about what she needed and desired.

> *The Lion* represented Dorothy's belief in her ability to defeat her fears and develop the courage to face obstacles along the way.

With her transformation complete, Dorothy soon grew into her own power and could reckon with any force that came her way. She could face whatever the Wicked Witch of the West threw at her—fireballs, flying monkeys, and all. Nothing could stop her! And yet, through it all, Dorothy was still Dorothy. Nothing about Dorothy had changed *except her beliefs!*

Removing the Mask

The process of changing our beliefs continues automatically throughout our lives, when we are true to our authentic self. Through this process we can believe ourselves into a better, more authentic life, but we have to choose this path by continuing to lead with our psychological rather than our social selves. The key is to not let what others think about us determine what we think about ourselves and to continue to present ourselves to the world as we truly are.

The great psychological theorist Carl Rogers called the reconciliation between who we are and whom we present ourselves to be "congruence"—a fit between the psychological and social or public persona. Once we have congruence, we become what Rogers called fully functioning individuals—well-adjusted and balanced, with hearts and minds working together in a harmonious way. Every thought, feeling, and action that we choose takes into account every facet of our being.

As fully functioning individuals, we are comfortable in our own skin. We've often heard this phrase, but now we *feel* it. Our bodies no longer just act as vessels; they become part of the complete picture of who we are—psychological, physical, and emotional. As we move through our lives in this new, balanced way, even though we still want success and happiness from the things that life can offer, suddenly it is no longer our sole reason to be. We are more focused on the continued unfolding of ourselves through the events of our lives. Truly, there is no place like home when we reach this stage of self-assurance with who we are.

Our beliefs can direct our course, for good and ill, which is why it's important that we stay on top of them, continuing to check and re-check what we believe to be true against our authentic way of being. We have to continue to strip away the illusions, maintaining reality and the sense of comfort with ourselves that we have worked so hard to gain. We have a brighter future before us, but we are solely responsible for bringing it to light.

The truth is, our beliefs continue to offer us the greatest opportunity for growth and change. *The key is to know which beliefs further our travels and which shut them down.* Are we small and meek? We are if we believe we are. Are we great and powerful? We are if we believe we are. Our beliefs can either move us forward or get us stuck. They can limit our learning and growth toward our true selves, or they can open up the power of our imagination and allow us to dream of a land over the rainbow that expresses our true selves.

Moving On with the Mindset of a Wizard

Several years ago at a conference on resilience, I met a young woman who was a newly minted professor at a major university. We spent some time talking about authentic development, and she shared with me the many ways in which she had worked hard to achieve her own goals. She had apparently started life with many disadvantages, yet she had risen above these obstacles, creating the life she had imagined for herself. She was very proud of this accomplishment, as well she should have been.

Our conversation continued in this positive light, but then she got very quiet. I could see she wanted to ask me something important. She looked at me so pensively and said something that I have never forgotten: "Debbie, I wonder sometimes if all of the emotional growing I have done has been worth it. I'm so emotionally far away from my family now, and have lost so many old friends. Sure, I've met new friends and my journey has opened up a whole other world for me. But I do feel the loss sometimes. Honestly, sometimes I wonder if it was a good or a bad thing to grow and change as I have done. What do you think?"

I knew exactly what she was feeling and have questioned the worth of the journey myself from time to time. Building a life that expresses who we truly are is never going to be easy. At times, the road to authentic development can be lonely and difficult—I had seen this firsthand, experiencing many losses of my own. Yet regardless of these losses, I have always felt that the effort was worth it. The truth is, I was hooked. I had bitten into the apple of authentic development and nothing would taste as satisfying to me ever again.

Yet we have to be prepared for the challenges that are likely to come. Once we start down this road, loved ones may no longer understand. They may wonder why we have given so much of our lives to finding our authentic selves. We may be thought of as having fanciful ideas or wasting our lives on meaningless pursuits. It can be a struggle to share our inner world with those we feel would not understand us. We are fortunate if we have one or two family members or friends who have also dared to take the journey to their authentic selves.

I shared these feelings with the young professor, but I knew she would have to decide upon the worth of the journey for herself. She was at a critical stage of psychological development (and on the road to Oz) in which she was beginning to question the purpose and meaning of the journey. Her question was a good sign that she was becoming well prepared for the changes that were still to come.

The Burden of Self-Knowledge

We have come far enough in our psychological growth to see who we truly are, but there are definite benefits and drawbacks that become readily apparent the moment we set foot in Oz. We know or should know by now all of the benefits derived from reaching this level of self-knowledge. Yet, it won't hurt at this point to clearly spell out both the positives and negatives associated with our journey—the joys and the burdens of reaching this level of psychological development. First, the negatives:

➤ We may make others in our lives uncomfortable, especially those who haven't taken the journey to Oz along with us.

➤ We now have the burden that comes with total self-reliance.

➤ We must take responsibility for making authentic choices, now that we know the difference.

> We will be called on to preserve, protect, and even sometimes defend our fragile new identity.

And the positives:

> We are at peace, grounded in our true selves.

> We have found something far greater than the world's opinion—the ability to be completely at home within ourselves.

> In terms of jobs, relationships, or other activities, we are now less likely to settle, and more likely to strive.

For me, there is no contest—the cost of remaining in Oz is worth a lifetime of personal fulfillment. I have seen this borne out over the years, watching so many individuals connect with their authentic selves, unable to turn back. The greater the strides made in finding our own way in life, the harder it becomes to turn our backs on our true selves. It's true. The more time that we spend in Oz, the greater the likelihood that we will stick around.

Trusting Ourselves

Moving on with the mindset of a wizard means trusting ourselves to come up with the right answers. People all around us may try to dissuade us from our true path. We have to maintain a firm commitment to ourselves to not go any way but our own. In Ralph Waldo Emerson's famous essay "On Self-Reliance,"he reminds us why this level of self-trust is essential. Emerson wrote that when we trust ourselves we avoid conformity and what he referred to as "false consistency" simply to retain a place in the world. We resist the pressure to sacrifice our individuality for the sake of fitting in or making other people happy. Emerson writes, "To be yourself in a world that is constantly trying to make you something else is the greatest accomplishment."

Of course, it is only by continually measuring everything against what we know to be true that we are able to resist the urge to conform. This is even trickier in our own time than it was in Emerson's due to the vast number of ideas and influences we are exposed to each day. Yet it is possible. The great benefit of our new way of being is that, even within the group, we are still free to be exactly who we are. That is because we run everything we see and hear through our newly constructed self-filter. This allows us to share the ideas and beliefs of the group, *but only by choice.*

For example, suppose we have read someone's opinion on a Facebook page. We may find it interesting and provocative, but even if we know the person well, we must examine this opinion to make sure it resonates with what we know to be true for ourselves. We may adopt the opinion, and even pass it on to others, but only by our own choice. We don't need to ask around to see whether or not others agree with the opinion. We don't need anyone's validation; we trust ourselves.

When we trust ourselves we are largely self-reliant. We do not *need* to identify with or gain the approval of any individual or group. We can still socialize and be part of the crowd, yet maintain our personal integrity.

Expressing Ourselves in the World

The philosophy of Ayn Rand exposes us to her theory of "objectivism," which represents, in its simplest terms, extreme creative potential, but also man standing alone against the world. In *The Fountainhead,* a brilliant architect named Howard Roark ultimately chooses total obscurity rather than compromise his artistic and individual vision. But Roark's fixed vision does not allow him to change or modify his beliefs, and within the course of Rand's work, Roark remains essentially the same: true to his vision, yet psychologically unchanged.

I prefer to think of our goal of getting to Oz in different terms. Although what is required is great depth of character and vision, I also see the importance of flexibility and changing our beliefs to allow psychological needs to unfold. We can and should remain true to our authentic selves; but life in Oz is not simply a matter of walking off to the beat of our own drummer. It is about drumming our own tune *while we exist in the world,* making ourselves count for something while retaining our integrity, ideals, and opinions.

I believe we can be ourselves and have room for others—but only those who don't require us to compromise our beliefs. Ultimately, it all begins by having continued faith in our selves. If we don't deliver for ourselves, then nothing much will happen to change our lives.

Staying in Oz

We have battled our way to Oz. We are welcome to remain there as long as we are content to watch ourselves grow and approach life from the vantage point of psychological curiosity. There will always be new things to learn about ourselves to further our development. The possibilities are as infinite as the yellow brick road that led us here and still stretches out before us.

The whole point of our journey has been to show us we are capable of so much more than we thought. We all have gifts that are important and special, and have only to learn how to use them. Even the Wizard knew that true wisdom, heart, and courage had only to be demonstrated to prove their existence. That is why he bestowed upon the Scarecrow the highest degree of Th.D. (Doctor of Thinkology); the Tin Man, a watch that ticked like a human heart; and the Lion, the Triple Cross, a medal that signified great courage. These were just tokens of course, for the Wizard knew, and we should too by now, it is what we believe about ourselves and what we do in the world that shows who we really are.

So, now that we have arrived in Oz, how do we stay there? We stay there by continuing to make the choices that validate our authentic way of being and standing up for our true selves. We stay there by continually adapting and changing our beliefs according to each new level of psychological development reached. And we stay there by continuing to follow the yellow brick road in our minds and hearts, allowing our hard-won psychological understanding to continue to lead us forward.

Chapter Nine:
Over the Rainbow

We have taken a daring journey. Like the mythical figure Hermes, the Greek god of transitions and boundaries, we have ferried fearlessly through the inner parts of ourselves to discover all that was there—the good and the bad—the hidden strengths, talents, abilities, fears, and emotional conflicts. At last we're in Oz where we can live without fear as authentic beings.

Our discoveries have brought into our psychological awareness the ability to act with full intention and the knowledge of who we are. We have found the rainbow within, the place that exists only through our own insight and imagination. Now we have a *living* place inside of us. It will continue to be our source of self-knowledge, intuitive wisdom, creativity, and strength.

Over the rainbow we are, in a sense, reborn. We have shed our social selves and become our real selves. We are comfortable now, but not so comfortable that we are passive. Being in Oz allows us to willingly participate in our own lives. Now we are able to gauge the meanings of the things that happen to us, taking our cues from inside us rather than from the outside world. Over the rainbow, we finally and completely engage with life through our true selves.

Full Circle

In the words of The Beatles, we are "back to where we once belonged," able to live our lives in authentic ways. But being in Oz doesn't mean that we lock ourselves up in isolation. We don't want to turn away from the ideas, beliefs, and thinking of others in the world. On the contrary—in Oz we live well, which means including others in our process. Oz becomes for us an instrument for self-reflection and self-evaluation—the lens through which we now see everything before us. We are fully in Oz and fully in the world.

Here is the difference between our lives *before* Oz and our lives *now*: *Before,* we were solely acting out of our social selves. We tended to let the ideas of the group influence our actions, without even considering their soundness. *Now,* we feel comfortable questioning ideas, even those we have heard for years and accepted as truth. We even reject ideas we had previously taken for granted.

Take, for example, the common phrase: A leopard doesn't change its spots. Before Oz, hearing this phrase might have caused us to accept it at face value, without giving it much thought. Now, we might stop and think about what this phrase really means: People don't change. *Really?* Well, now that we ourselves have changed, we know this isn't true. We might re-evaluate and say, "No. People *can* change, given the right circumstances."

Now that there is a place inside of us that we are aware of and comfortable enough to live in, we have the chance to decide things for ourselves. No longer do we need to rely on the outside world to tell us how things are. We just *know* how things are. This doesn't mean that we throw out all that we have learned or disregard what other's think. It's just that going forward we evaluate and re-evaluate our ideas and beliefs to see how they fit with what we are learning and the way our life is taking shape. We are likely to turn away from ideas that have little relevance to our journey.

Going forward, we find ourselves picking and choosing, then keeping or discarding, refusing to live anyone else's journey but our own. We are always in receiving mode, yet simultaneously able to sort relevant from irrelevant facts as we sift through the barrage of information that assaults our senses. We may question what is brought to our attention, but we never question who *we* are and what *we* believe.

Holding Our Own

In Shel Silverstein's *The Missing Piece*, a lonely circle searches the world over for the piece of himself that is missing and that will complete him. He finally discovers his missing piece, but soon learns that becoming a complete circle does not fulfill him. It was his rough edges that gave him the ability to keep on rolling along, learning new things and growing. It was the journey, and not the destination, that made him whole.

The truth is, without a search, without our rough edges, we lose our purpose and external goals and, ultimately, lose our way. Too much smoothness and satisfaction blocks exchange with the outside world and prevents us from continuing to grow. Of course, this was never our goal in getting to Oz. We want to continue to grow and change and let our rough edges show. It is these rough edges that lead us into a special way of being in the world that is unique and authentic to us.

In Oz we always aim for the satisfaction that comes from achieving a state of wholeness—all of our parts working together so that we are able to act in authentic ways. We seek satisfaction in all we do, but—and here's the important thing—*we do not stop ourselves from doing*. It is, of course, gratifying to reach a place of peace and fulfillment. We all need points of rest and relaxation in our lives. But there is such a thing as Polynesian Paralysis—a slowing of life that eventually turns us from beings into objects. We don't ever want to feel as if there's nothing left for us to learn, as if our lives are perfect.

Naturally, the more time that we spend in Oz, the more we are likely to experience periods of inner peace and enjoyment. Thank goodness for that. But we need our rough edges to nudge us out of complacency and into the searching process once again. In Oz, we keep our experiences ongoing and varied, never permitting ourselves to fall to a zero point of motivation. We know that too much satisfaction, or a sense of completeness, may block us from exchanges with the outside world.

Our goal in getting to Oz was never perfection, but to keep our selves fully engaged in the *process* of living. This process is an ongoing effort to tie up loose ends, resolve inner conflicts, and fulfill goals. We continuously move toward an ideal view of what it means to live in the world and use our time well. Now that we are fully awake, grounded in our ruby slippers and vitally alive, we know what life is truly about—not perfection or completion, but an ongoing process of alertness and aliveness.

Being Alive

In Oz, it is our psychological momentum that keeps us engaged in the world. Our hearts and minds are always directed toward future possibilities that exist outside ourselves. We hold our own not through stagnation but by keeping ourselves open to exchanges with the world so that we can keep on learning and growing. We do this even in the face of challenging circumstances that threaten our authentic sense of self. We know leading an authentic life means we welcome change, using it to fuel new growth and aliveness.

I remember well what the great basketball player Magic Johnson said when he first learned he was HIV positive: "Don't feel sorry for me." Simple words, but I believe what Magic was trying to convey was something important about fulfillment and the ideal life. He understood that it isn't the completion of our dreams that makes our life worth living. It is using the time we have left on earth as well as we possibly can, even in the face of adversity. It is *being alive.*

Magic Johnson's tragic career-ending illness moved him into Oz, where his new psychological awareness allowed him to move on to other causes. No longer able to use his talent and energy to play basketball, he dedicated himself to heightening the public's awareness of AIDS. He went on to build a foundation to create funds for more AIDS research. He did not dwell on his illness. Instead, he used it as a starting point for sweeping change in his life.

The greatest gift of our journey to Oz is that we now know how to be alive; we know what is worthwhile spending time on and what is not; and we know that no matter what happens, it is important to go forward. Once in Oz it is impossible to go backward; we cannot reverse the psychological process that has brought us here or the positive changes in our lives that are taking place. We make the best of where we are right here, right now, knowing that in our special state of heart, mind, and spirit, our rough edges can flourish.

Satisfaction may exist in Oz, but beyond it there are still

adventures to be had, missing pieces to explore. We pick them up along the way, using them not to complete ourselves but to continue the process of growth that still lies before us.

The New Social Self

At last we are comfortable in our ruby slippers, seated firmly in our own power. It has taken a lot of personal growth and change to get to where we are right now. We've come a long way and are now psychologically mature enough to allow a great shift to take place. Now, in this stunning place of comfort and security, we can act out of our true desires and needs. What is more, we can now wish for everyone the comfort and personal freedom that comes from having taken this precious journey to Oz. This is how it feels to be our new social self.

Our new social self is generous. It can afford to be! It looks and feels strong enough to let the desires and needs of others ride along with its own. Once our social self had to be very self-focused to find its way out of the tornado and onto the road to Oz. Now that we have satisfied our basic needs and committed to an authentic way of life, our new social self is defined and strong enough to not only handle its own needs and desires, but to allow itself to be concerned about the needs and desires of others.

In our new social self, we begin to cultivate a state of awareness that expresses our relationship to other individuals as psychological beings, each of us standing side by side trying to unfold authenticity and true purpose. As partners in Oz we have developed such a mutual respect for the journey, that we are able to stand together, each of us holding our own, while allowing the other to do the same.

It is the policy of the new social self to live and let live. We never fear that others will get ahead faster than we will or have more than we do. We don't have to tear other individuals down to make ourselves feel good. We have psychologically and spiritually evolved to the point that we can strive and let others strive too. So what if other people get ahead of us, have more, or differ in their beliefs and values? This no longer threatens or consumes us, as it has no relevance in Oz, where each of us gets an equal shot at fulfillment.

In Oz we finally *get* that authentic development isn't about ridding ourselves of people, moving alone to mountaintops, or shedding all desire for emotional closeness. *We still need others!* Oz is also not a place in which our beliefs and values are the only right ones just because we have taken the journey there. This journey is about joy and inclusiveness, the twin spirits that pervade our lives over the rainbow.

A Love Song

To know if we are really in Oz, there's no better test than to ask ourselves this question: How do we feel about others? If we are truly in Oz, we want nothing more than for others to join us here. Our new social self wants to let people in on this magical transformation, not deprive them of it.

Think of how generously Dorothy invited the Scarecrow, the Tin Woodman, and the Lion to join her on her journey to Oz. Oz inspires us in this way, making us want to give back, to share with others all that we have learned—our successes and even our failures that we have picked up along the way. We only have to have made the visit to Oz ourselves to know that what lies here is precious and that it belongs to everyone, not just ourselves. We know too that Oz is a journey we can only experience for ourselves.

In T. S. Eliot's *The Love Song of J Alfred Prufrock*, a man in the later stages of his life tells a listener, "Oh, do not ask 'What is it.' Let us go and make our visit." You cannot tell another individual what it is like in Oz; they have to see it for themselves. That's because being in Oz not only changes what is inside us, but how we see things—subtle details such as those in Eliot's poem— "the yellow fog that rubs its back on the window-panes" or "the women [who] come and go." In Oz, we experience a rich inner feeling that allows us to notice such details but not to share them. To appreciate the full power of the ruby slippers, we must all go and "make the visit," or take the journey to Oz.

For the World, Not of It

After we have spent some time in Oz we begin to open ourselves up again to the world. We find that we are now more intrigued by people than we were before. We notice that despite our uniqueness, we are more alike than different from other people. We no longer fear people from other backgrounds, cultures, and religions, because we know at our core we are all the same; people striving to understand themselves and to understand each other, to give and get respect, and to have a chance to live the best life possible.

Naturally, it is a continual challenge not to measure ourselves against all that we see around us and instead keep our ideal vision for our lives as we find our way. But the more time we spend in Oz, the more we manage to do this. It is as if we develop a protective armor that shields us from social pressure and enables us to resist being swayed by mass opinion. We root for what is going on around us, and we remain open to exchanges with the world; yet we retain our individuality.

In the film *Gladiator,* a senator vying for a democratic versus an autocratic system declares himself as being "for the world but not of it." Yes, that is exactly the way we must think of ourselves in Oz. As a result of our stay here, we are no longer *of* the world, but we are most definitely still *for* it. We have found a place of comfort and maturity, yet we refuse to close ourselves off. We have armor to protect us, but not to isolate us.

In fact, we reach out to the world in all the ways that we can. Once in Oz, a new spirit of generosity and inclusiveness claims us. This spirit gets passed on, and before long, we find ourselves surrounded by a community of like-minded travelers and soon-to-be travelers to Oz, all resonating to the same spirit. As we continue to grow and learn from one another, we rise even higher. By letting others back in, we attain the highest spirit Oz has to offer.

All the Colors of the Rainbow

The road to Oz has given us great rewards, but also a few

surprises. Perhaps the biggest surprise of all was to find—as did the great Oz himself—that our strength lies not in who we are or what we have, but in what we know how to give. In Oz we become concerned with the difference we can make via a commitment to and connection with the next generation.

Before arriving in Oz, many of us were giving, caring individuals who sought to make a difference in the lives of others. The difference is, once in Oz, we no longer think of it in terms of "giving back" or "making a contribution." We just know it is something we *have* to do. In the natural course of our daily lives we are always thinking of new ways to help others. We give even more than we get. We leave our mark on the world, but this is only as a result of our efforts and not our true purpose.

Everyday Wizards

In purely psychological terms, being in Oz fits neatly into psychologist Erik Erikson's stages of psychosocial development. Erikson described the seventh stage of development as "generativity," corresponding with a time in our lives when, having achieved an authentic life vision, we turn to the ways in which we can pass on what we know to the next generation. Generativity involves the struggle to create a living legacy, whether through having children or caring in some other way for others. For each of us in Oz, the path to generativity produces a different result, unique to our own talents and abilities. For me, it produced something more beautiful than I could ever have imagined.

I had been working as a clinical psychologist in private practice for several years. Even though I had made my own journey to Oz, there was still conflict in my life—the rough edges were still there—yet gradually I had begun to feel that my concerns were not going to be solved in isolation; they were in some way intricately connected to the concerns of others.

But let me step back a bit. When I began my practice, it was difficult for me to accept payment for my services. I believed that it was each person's right to psychologically develop, and not a privilege only meant for people who have the resources to grow into their full potential. Yet, I was forced to adhere to the tenets of my profession that required psychologists to be paid for services rendered, even if only nominal amounts. Once in Oz, I found myself eager to find a way to share the benefits of my journey, even with those who could not afford the high fees of my clinical practice.

One day it came to me; I knew what I had to do. If individuals could not afford to come to me, I would go to them; I would give psychology away! The seed of an idea took shape, and over time, it matured and blossomed into the start of my Internet blog/publication *Psychology in Everyday Life*, which resulted in the book that you are reading today. Now, not only was I helping others to thrive, they were sharing their stories, ideas, beliefs, and blessings with many others. Followers from all over the world—of every country, religion, culture, and background—were not only reading my blog, they were interacting with me on a daily basis. As I passed the message of Oz along, I received much more than I could possibly ever give in return.

The Grand Plan

Like Dorothy and her friends, each of us sets out for Oz hoping for great changes in our lives. What we learn when we arrive here is that the talents and skills that we have been granted aren't just for us after all, but for the greater good. In Oz, it all works out the same, whether we are on the giving or receiving end. We are all part of a grand plan, far greater than the goals and desires that brought us here. This is what allows us to stay in Oz, where we continue to learn and grow.

And isn't that the point after all—to tap our heels together three times and rise as high as we possibly can? This is what we have been searching for our whole lives, down below and then way up high, over the rainbow—a place of deep personal renewal, where we could live without fear. In Oz, we have found it. At last we are home.

ABOUT THE AUTHOR

Dr. Deborah Khoshaba has emerged as one of the leading psychologists in her area of work. Her groundbreaking research on coping and resilience strategies as part of The Hardiness Institute initiative has earned her tremendous accolades within the academic community, and her books published on the subject continue to enjoy wide critical acclaim. Over the course of her 25-year clinical career, she has treated over a thousand patients suffering from a wide range of conditions, including marital problems, eating disorders, posttraumatic stress disorder at the military level, and emergencies at the public service level. Many have returned to work with her at multiple points in their lives.

As impressive as Dr. Khoshaba's CV is, it is not nearly as compelling as the story of who she is:

Deborah Khoshaba grew up in Chicago, Illinois, born into a family of six children of two working, immigrant parents. Early in life, she found herself drawn to music and followed that passion into her first career as a professional opera singer. It was through the experience of performing live before an audience at the Chicago Lyric Opera that Deborah discovered the enormous communicative power of music; its ability to uplift and transform, offering thousands of listeners a brief moment of respite from the varied complexities or irrevocable sorrows of their everyday lives.

Relief and comfort, Deborah decided, are the greatest gifts that can be given or received.

It was this perspective on the world, developed through a cultural lens, that later shaped Dr. Deborah's philosophy as a psychologist. The breadth of her emotional range developed through the arts, coupled with an ability to recognize parallels and relatable themes in seemingly disparate contexts, has served to greatly magnify Dr. Deborah's value throughout her career and has led to numerous successes, academic and commercial. Her work continues to appeal equally to the specialized academic community, and to the greater mainstream public.

Through the use of film therapy, music, and literary analysis (as well as other creative metaphors and allegories), Dr. Deborah has brought intuitive depth and dimension to her work as a therapist that continues to resonate profoundly with her patients, students, and readers.

In 2008, while a professor at the University of California, Irvine, she was voted Teacher of the Year by over 300 students. An accomplished author, she has penned two books and countless articles for esteemed academic publications.

A strong and engaging performer noted for her natural warmth, Dr. Deborah has been a series regular on various radio and educational television programs. In 2009, she was selected as the host of Journey on VoiceAmerica, a live call-in show where she offered on-the-air clinical advice. In 2012, Dr. Deborah was chosen as lead psychologist as part of the core cast for *Shrink Rap*, a reality television pilot by On Purpose Productions.

Her blog *Get Hardy* on *Psychology Today* continues to gain popularity, while Dr. Deborah's empathetic voice already reaches over 150,000 dedicated readers who visit her Facebook page as well as her monthly blog, *Psychology in Everyday Life,* in search of compassion and advice.

23689245R00087

Made in the USA
Middletown, DE
31 August 2015